ECHOES OF ETERNITY

Listening to the Father

VOLUME TWO

Hal M. Helms

PARACLETE PRESS
Brewster, Massachusetts

Unless otherwise designated, Scripture quotations are taken from the King James
Version of the Bible.

Scripture quotations designated (NIV) are taken from the Holy Bible, New International
Version ®. NIV ®. Copyright © 1973, 1978, 1984 by International Bible Society. Used
by permission of Zondervan Publishing House. All rights reserved.

Library of Congress Cataloging-in-Publication Data
    Echoes of eternity: listening to the Father.
    p. cm.
    ISBN 1-55725-173-8 (alk. paper)
    1. Devotional calendars. I. Paraclete Press.

BV4810.E24   1996
242'.2—dc20   96-24801
                                       CIP

10 9 8 7 6 5 4 3 2 1

© 1998 by The Community of Jesus, Inc.
ISBN#: 1-55725-206-8

Published by Paraclete Press,
Brewster, Massachusetts
www.paraclete-press.com
Printed in the United States of America

Introduction

On August 15, 1997, just one week before our fifty-fifth wedding anniversary, the Lord had need of my husband Hal and called him home. His death was not totally unexpected for he had been gravely ill for several years, but its time and manner were a surprise. Hal was in the hospital awaiting gall bladder surgery when he took a drastic turn for the worse and suddenly died.

Nine months have now passed and I find I miss Hal more and more as time goes on. But grace has been abundant, and I can honestly say I wouldn't bring him back for anything. Death and the grave are past, and Hal has been mercifully delivered from the pain he lived with constantly for years. I identify with King David who said, on the death of his son, "He will not return to me but I will go to him."

A few months after Hal's death, his spiritual director and his editor asked me if I would put together a second volume of *Echoes of Eternity*. Indeed, Hal had wanted to compile a second volume but had not had the time. As I began to work with these messages I found that Jesus was using them to bless and comfort me in my grief. The personal nature of some of the words prevents them from being made public, so with this second volume, we have now exhausted the messages Hal recorded in his journals and treasured as he faithfully kept his early morning appointments with the Lord.

I know many readers have been blessed and uplifted by the first volume of *Echoes of Eternity*. I trust you will find *Echoes of Eternity, Volume II* a support for your faith and an encouragement in your daily walk with Jesus. God bless you, and may your life be lived with joy and zest until you take up residence in your Heavenly home.

Helen Helms
April 22, 1998

JANUARY

Morning has broken like the first morning,
   Blackbird has spoken like the first bird.
Praise for the singing! Praise for the morning!
   Praise for them, springing fresh from the Word!

Sweet the rain's new fall sunlit from heaven,
   Like the first dewfall on the first grass.
Praise for the sweetness of the wet garden,
   Sprung in completeness where His feet pass.

Mine is the sunlight! Mine is the morning
   Born of the one light Eden saw play!
Praise with elation, praise every morning,
   God's re-creation of the new day!

Eleanor Farjeon, 1881-1965

January First

The children of men take refuge in the shadow of Thy wings.
Psalm 36:7b

This is a day of reckoning. I do not mean this twenty-four hour period, but this time in which you are living. Reckoning means squaring accounts. Reckoning means settling up. And that is what this period is in your life. Remember, however, that My tender mercies are over all My works—and this is especially true when I require reckoning of My servants.

My hand is stretched out to bless, not to curse you. There is nothing to fear—all is intended to bring growth in the Spirit.

January Second

Where sin increased, grace abounded all the more, so that, as sin reigned in death, grace also might reign through righteousness to eternal life through Jesus Christ our Lord.
Romans 5:20b-21

Why are you cast down, My son, in these peaceful circumstances around you? Why do you linger over hurts and jealousies, when My peace and My joy are yours? Old sin patterns die hard—but they *do* die if that is the desire of your heart.

January Third

For Thou, O Lord, art my hope, my trust, O Lord, from my youth.

Psalm 71:5

My son, I have not abandoned you. In your fear you felt cut off and alone. But I was there, and will be there no matter what your feelings tell you. Yes, I am speaking to you. This is not a construct of your wishful thinking.

You wonder what purpose could be served in such an experience as you had. First, you must learn to be more obedient. You give in much too easily to feelings of tiredness. Second, you must learn to bring your thoughts into captivity to My Sovereign Spirit. You were not at all successful night before last. "The years the locusts have eaten"—are much, very much, involved here.

Be of good courage. All is not lost. Only pride and shallow faith—but what are they?

January Fourth

Behold, to obey is better than sacrifice.

I Samuel 15:22b

Listen to Me instead of your own thoughts. Your thoughts are full of anxiety and fear, fantasy and unreality. My thoughts are not as yours. That is why a person is kept in "perfect peace" when the mind is stayed on Me.

I know your circumstances—and your physical needs. My arm is not shortened that it cannot save—and I am the Lord who healeth thee. How many times have I told you before, yet you grovel in shadows and self-pity. Your pain is but for a season—and it is never without amelioration. So do not magnify it beyond what it is. Have a good day in spite of it by listening to Me instead of your thoughts. Remember, "Whoso offereth praise glorifieth Me." So offer praise continually through the day.

January Fifth

The Lord preserves the simple.

Psalm 116:6a

Look unto Me, My child. Gaze steadily upon My mercy. Know that you are a child of mercy—and that the blessings I pour out on you are the fruit of mercy. Long you have wandered afield, gazing on the things of the world, pulled by the attraction of things that perish and fade. It is time, high time, to fix your gaze on heavenly things. Seek the incorruptible crown, My son. Let go your burning desire to "be somebody" and accept the lowly and despised place I will for you. Look unto Me—and keep looking.

January Sixth

I am the good shepherd; I know My own and My own know Me.

John 10:14

This quiet time is My gift of love to you, My son. In spite of the multitude of distractions, it still carries the stamp of My blessing. You are receiving more than you know. Healing is taking place, fallow ground is being broken up, and the holy seed of My truth is being planted. As you see the snow gently falling to the waiting ground, so My mercies descend on your waiting soul—quietly, without noise or fanfare. This is My way.

January Seventh

If we live by the Spirit, let us also walk by the Spirit.

Galatians 5:25

I know your impatience in waiting—your desire to have a quick and verifying word from Me. Think, My son, is this the right attitude with which to approach the eternal Majesty on high? Is it not rather a symptom of your great self-love and demanding nature? Why must you wait to hear My voice? Because of this very aspect which you bring to these meetings, our communication is impeded.

I do not rebuke you harshly, but appeal to you as a loving Father: Learn to be content with waiting when I seem to delay in speaking. Learn that in the silence much is to be gained if you let it work for you.

Do not lose your grateful heart for these moments—they are *not* ordinary. Don't let their frequency blind you to their incomparable worth to your soul.

January Eighth

For He has made known to us in all wisdom and insight the mystery of His will . . . to unite all things in Him, things in heaven and things on earth.

Ephesians 1:9-10

My word brings joy even when it causes you pain. It brings life, even when it brings death to your wonted ways. Rather, it brings joy *because* it brings pain, and life *because* it brings death.

The deepest things of life remain a mystery to you, My child, and it must be so. In the mystery there are realities as yet only faintly grasped or dimly seen. But their presence assures you that there is more to life with Me than you have yet experienced.

Do not be afraid of the mysteries, and do not try to explain them away. This foolish effort on your part has robbed you of blessings and stunted your growth in Me for many years. Expand the capacity of your soul to admit what you cannot understand or reason out—and let My word bring the life and joy you so much want and need.

January Ninth

My eyes are toward Thee, O Lord God; in Thee I seek refuge; leave me not defenseless!

Psalm 141:8

This is My word to you today: Repent of who you are, and let My Spirit convict you of who you are in particular areas of need. Do not frustrate My design by looking for a quick and *painless* fix—but *believe* that I am accomplishing that which I have begun in you.

January Tenth

O Thou who hearest prayer! To Thee shall all flesh come.

Psalm 65:2

I hear your prayer, and it shall be done. No prayer is prayed in vain. Leave the particulars to Me, My child, and in My time and way your desire will be fulfilled. I am still training you in the path of faith. I still look for trust rather than doubt or questioning. A loving relationship must be built on trust—and you have ample ground for that, do you not? So keep on praying and *learning* that trust is a choice which you can make. Don't let doubts discourage you. Let My strength encourage your fearful heart.

January Eleventh

Do you not know that God's kindness is meant to lead you to repentance?

Romans 2:4b

Vain regret is not repentance. Yes, you have made *many* wrong choices through the course of your life. But I have no pleasure in the self-pity of remorse. Since My grace has never been lacking and My mercy has never been withdrawn from you, your life has been a redeemed life. It does not mean that the wrong choices brought no harm—they did and do. But My grace has been and is greater, and those choices did not overrule it.

My gift of repentance, unlike vain regret, is a forward-looking attitude. It enables you to lay hold of My future, cleansed and freed from paralyzing guilt and shame. Claim it, My child, and let your tears be tears of joy and gratitude.

January Twelfth

Blessed are the merciful, for they shall obtain mercy.

Matthew 5:7

I am the Lord your God. I am with you in your present condition and will be with you always. Let your feeble faith be strengthened and enlarged to rejoice in My sure love. I am the same yesterday, today and forever. I change not, and *never* forsake those whom I love. Be at peace and drive away foolish fantasies and fears.

January Thirteenth

And I am sure that He who began a good work in you will bring it to completion at the day of Jesus Christ.

Philippians 1:6

My dear child, I have missed these quiet meetings with you. You see, I know how much you need Me, how much you need the reassurance of My love, and how dark your way becomes when you neglect your relationship with Me. I am your *light*. I am your *hope*. I am your *strength* and *defense*. You can never face the enemy with his wiles and deceptions on your own. Remember that.

In addition, remember too that My love calls you to a fellowship of love. This is a "two-way street"—and you greatly misjudge the reality of it when you think your neglect has no effect on Me. I hope you will not forget this.

January Fourteenth

Therefore, my brethren, whom I love and long for, my joy and crown, stand firm thus in the Lord, my beloved.

Philippians 4:1

My dear child, do not be dismayed at the various trials you are experiencing. They are being used for purposes you cannot see nor understand at this point in your life. Only trust My unfailing goodness. When the waters overwhelm you, remember then My past faithfulness and flee inwardly to Me. Your pattern is still to withdraw into yourself—isolated and cut off from Me and from others. The fear and feeling of panic have *driven* you to admit your need and seek others. That is a *good* result, even though you are humiliated by it.

January Fifteenth

Do nothing from selfishness or conceit, but in humility count others better than yourselves.

Philippians 2:3

My dear child, I have given you, out of My tender mercies, *many* of your heart's desires. You should recollect and give thanks for the manifold display of My great goodness to you. I know your weaknesses and failings. I am acquainted with all your imperfections and sin. But I see you, in My beloved Son, as you will one day be by My grace.

The sufferings through which you pass are as much expressions of My mercy as the heart's desires that I have granted you. Bless Me in them all and be blessed.

January Sixteenth

And whenever you stand praying, forgive, if you have anything against anyone; so that your Father also who is in heaven may forgive you your trespasses.

Mark 11:25

This is My word to you today, My child. Be forthright in what you say and take care in the way you walk. Trust Me in every uncertainty, for in trusting your soul is further healed.

Forgive the wrongs done or said against you, for in forgiving you rob them of their power to hurt.

You are My care, and I have not forgotten to be gracious. Do not forget to be thankful!

January Seventeenth

We know that in everything God works for good with those who love Him, who are called according to His purpose.

Romans 8:28

The storms of life are necessary for the clearing of the soul. The debris of sin beclouds your vision and hinders the ongoing progress of My purpose. The present storm is but a small one which I am allowing for this purpose. Let the clearer air clarify your thoughts. Let the power of My purposes override the paucity of yours, and produce the fruit of My purposes. Then you will see how necessary was this storm.

January Eighteenth

They loved the praise of men more than the praise of God.

John 12:43

My dear child, I have waited these many years for you to come to this place. You, like the Jewish rulers who believed on Me, loved the praises of men more than the praise of God. How often I would have led you in another way. The inklings you felt—the momentary shafts of light and longing that penetrated your soul—were not accidental. They were gentle invitations for you to "Come away, My beloved. . . ."

I want you to grow in this new dimension—this inward listening to My still, small voice. I have supplied you with healthy balances to keep you from veering off in unsafe paths. Trust Me, My child—and keep on trusting—because without trust, you will flounder and fail.

January Nineteenth

And I will give them one heart, and put a new spirit within them; I will take the stony heart out of their flesh and give them a heart of flesh that they may walk in My statutes and keep My ordinances and obey them; and they shall be My people, and I will be their God.

Ezekiel 11:19-20

Yes, My son, My Spirit is sent forth to unite you with Me. Through this miracle, I extend My life and My very nature *into* the lives of My people. So then, you are participating in My life even when you know it not. Christ in you, the hope of glory. This is a mystery which you can believe without understanding and attempting to analyze. Rejoice, My dear child, in what you have been given. Rejoice in what you have been denied. Both are from Me, and are expressions of My love and goodness to you. That love will never run out, and the streams of My mercy will never run dry.

January Twentieth

Behold, I am with you and will keep you wherever you go, and will bring you back to this land; for I will not leave you until I have done that of which I have spoken to you.

Genesis 28:15

According to My loving kindness and tender mercy I have kept faith with you, My child. I am not one who forgets and neglects, and so I have been mindful of you and your needs even when these meetings have been neglected on your part. I do not want you to regard them as a burden but as a privilege without peer. You do not yet comprehend the mercy which I have showered on you, and are only dimly aware of how vital it is if you are to fulfill My call and My will for you. Be faithful in the little things. In them are the seed of the great ones.

January Twenty-first

Let us then with confidence draw near to the throne of grace, that we may receive mercy and find grace to help in time of need.

Hebrews 4:16

My dear son, you are troubled about many things—and about one thing: your fear of what lies ahead for you and your ability to cope with it. You do not have to cope alone—as you have seen in weeks past. I bid you be of good cheer. Let the promises work for you. Do not negate them by refusing to believe. Remember Israel in the wilderness. They did not enter in because of their unbelief. You do not need to make the same bad choice!

January Twenty-second

For I know the plans I have for you, says the Lord, plans for welfare and not for evil, to give you a future and a hope.

Jeremiah 29:11

In the year that lies ahead there will be many wonders. You will see My hand unmistakably at work in your midst. Flinch not before My judgments, and do not let the enemy's accusations lodge in your heart. Be patient under My rod, for it is for your eternal good. My goodness will not fail you and grace will always abound. Some will fall away, for they are not grounded in Me. Their going may bring pain, but it will bring no loss. There must be a deeper, firmer reliance on Me rather than on secondary causes. Pride must be dealt with or it will destroy what I have given. This is My word and I will fulfill it.

January Twenty-third

I have loved you with an everlasting love; therefore I have continued My faithfulness to you.

Jeremiah 31:3

My children, My children, I love you. My joy in you is not complete until you know and comprehend that love. It is a love that passes knowledge, and I invite you all to journey past mere knowledge into that fullness of love. Do not be afraid of love, My children. Be afraid rather of your closed, protective shells that shut out My sun. Do not be afraid of being kind to one another, of making allowances for weaknesses and wounds not yet fully healed. Beware of self-righteousness, for it bears bitter fruit. Sing and rejoice in the Love that sought and found you. It will not lead you astray.

January Twenty-fourth

Trust in the Lord, and do good; so you will dwell in the land, and enjoy security. Take delight in the Lord, and He will give you the desires of your heart.

Psalm 37:3-4

My light is shining on your way. My path is unfolding before you as you walk with Me. You do not need to see ahead, and it would be harmful to you if you could. My way and My wisdom are always best. Do not fear what lies on the path. The darkness will disappear at the right time, and you will see everything you need to see. No harm can come to the soul that is in My care. No harm can come to you as long as you stay with Me.

January Twenty-fifth

Now may the Lord of peace Himself give you peace at all times in all ways.

II Thessalonians 3:16

My dear son, I am still working out My purposes in your life. The mantle of My mercy is still over you. My goodness is your daily supply.

Walk in hope and truth. Be quick to confess your inward sin—avoid the trap of self-pity. My glory and mercy will yet be seen.

January Twenty-sixth

Behold, I am doing a new thing; now it springs forth, do you not perceive it? I will make a way in the wilderness and rivers in the desert.

Isaiah 43:19

Yes, My son, you need to listen—like Martha, you are busy about many things in your mind. I could overpower your thoughts if I chose, but I prefer to have you struggle to be quiet and make that an offering to Me. You will be more greatly blessed by that procedure. You see, do you not, that when you get your mind focused, you can hear and receive My word to you. Yet this focusing is easily lost to a straying thought if you do not guard it well.

January Twenty-seventh

Let your light so shine before men, that they may see your good works and give glory to your Father who is in heaven.

Matthew 5:16

Rest now with Me and in Me, My son, in the full assurance of My love. Abide in Me quietly and let this day be a quiet one for your soul. Much is accomplished in the hidden depths of a quiet heart.

January Twenty-eighth

And after the earthquake a fire, but the Lord was not in the fire; and after the fire a still small voice.

I Kings 19:12

Like light piercing through the darkness My Spirit pierces through the muddle of your mind and thoughts. They still form a dense thicket—and much pruning must be done.

My grace has been heavy upon you. Let your mind rest now on the *knowledge* that I love you and have accepted you as My child. You have far to go and grow in this basic truth.

January Twenty-ninth

Your ways and your doings have brought this upon you.

Jeremiah 4:18a

The wounds that you inflict upon your soul wound Me also. Remember this when you are tempted and drawn toward evil. Forbidden pleasures, even mental ones, are short-lived, but leave a residue of injury behind. Flee from these temptations to Me and abide in Me. Recognize the tactics of your adversary and do not play the fool!

January Thirtieth

Cast thy burden on the Lord, and He will sustain you; He will never permit the righteous to be moved.

Psalm 55:22

Go in My strength to the duties of the day. Stay close to Me in your heart, and you will know the communion of My Spirit. Walk in the light I give you in each situation, and know that I am with you to bless and guide. Fret not yourself over what "might be." I am still in charge and will give you what is best for you. This is My promise.

January Thirty-first

Is My hand shortened, that it cannot redeem? Or have I no power to deliver?

Isaiah 50:2b

Believe and you will see. Greater wonders will yet unfold. My arm is not shortened, and My purpose stands. I lead My flock in ways that seem strange to you. But I know the way and I know the destination to which I led you. I do not expect you to see or understand all. But I do ask you to believe. That is the strong cord binding heart to heart—believing, trusting. Against that the enemy has no power. But it is yours to choose. And I counsel you again, My child, "be not faithless—but believing."

FEBRUARY

How firm a foundation, ye saints of the Lord,
    Is laid for your faith in His excellent Word.
What more can He say than to you He hath said?
    To you who for refuge to Jesus have fled.

"Fear not, I am with you, Oh be not dismayed;
    For I am thy God and will still give thee aid.
I'll strengthen thee, help thee, and cause thee to stand
    Upheld by My righteous, omnipotent hand.

"When through fiery trials thy pathway shall lie,
    My grace, all sufficient, shall be thy supply.
The flames shall not hurt thee, I only design
    Thy dross to consume and thy gold to refine.

"When through the deep waters I call thee to go,
    The rivers of woe shall not thee overflow.
For I will be with thee, thy troubles to bless,
    And sanctify to thee thy deepest distress."

K. in Rippon's Selection, *1787*

February First

Oh give thanks to the Lord, for He is good; for His steadfast love endures forever!

I Chronicles 16:34

Thanks and praise become the upright. Thanks and praise become the sinner. Forgiveness begets a thankful heart. Never cease to lift your heart in grateful remembrance of what I have done for you, My child, for in this is your safeguard. Once the well of thankfulness goes dry or is clogged through misuse, disobedience is not far behind, and with it, all the sorrows and pain it entails; you *need* to practice praise. Your identity and welfare are intimately tied up in it. Praise is not a luxury. It is as vital as the air.

February Second

For God alone my soul waits in silence, for my hope is from Him.

Psalm 62:5

Expect a blessing—that is the faith attitude I am pleased with when you come to pray. You would not go repeatedly to someone with a request you did not *expect* to be received favorably. Likewise, My child, when you approach the throne of grace, I want that expectancy to flood your heart. With such sacrifice I am well pleased. The sacrifice involved is the laying down of your old fear-filled, guilt-laden thoughts. I have promised that those who *trust* in Me will not be confounded. So come to Me *expecting* a fulfillment of My word.

February Third

Then said Jesus, "Were not ten cleansed? Where are the nine? Was no one found to return and give praise to God except this foreigner?"
Luke 17:17-18

My greatness and My glory are seen in little things as well as great ones. For those with eyes to see, there is glory everywhere. With those who have ears to hear, there is the music of the spheres. Much of the chaos of this present world is rooted in the lust for bigger things. Blessed are those who find contentment in little things. Learn this lesson, My child, and be blessed.

February Fourth

O man of little faith, why did you doubt?

Matthew 14:31b

Never doubt My goodness. That is one of the chief ploys of your adversary—to insert questions in your mind about Me. He knows where to attack at the weak places in your spiritual armor—which are the "strong" places in yourself. What folly to allow his little game to triumph over you, when you have a Strong Deliverer! O My child, would that you would settle it once for all—that My goodness faileth never. I am who I am and I change not. Never, *never* doubt My goodness!

February Fifth

. . . *those who through faith and patience inherit the promises.*
Hebrews 6:12b

I have given you My word. My promises are sure. There is no turning or wavering in My heart. Turn your thoughts to this sure foundation so that *your* heart may also learn steadiness and steadfastness. Let us go on together, My child, in a relationship of loving trust. Let us go on with the sure knowledge I have given you, and let Me prove again and again that those who put their trust in Me shall not be confounded.

February Sixth

And you shall rejoice in the Lord; in the Holy One of Israel you shall glory.

Isaiah 41:16b

This is a day of blessing and mercy. Open your faith-eyes to behold both. It is My joy to shower goodness upon those who love Me and seek My face. My heart is ever toward them, to bring them new light and hope. My fatherly care is ever extended to them and they are kept by My sovereign power.

When you are attuned to My Spirit, you are under the overflow of My blessing and mercy. When you join with others who likewise seek My face, joy abounds. Have a joyful day!

February Seventh

Go; be it done for you as you have believed.

Matthew 8:13

Believing and receiving go hand in hand, My child. Just as the radio must be *tuned* to a certain frequency to pick up a particular broadcast, so, in a manner of speaking, must your heart be *attuned* to Me. Believing opens up your receiving capacity. Without it, you are shut off and have only your own thoughts and reasonings.

Because you have set such a high store on reasoning and being reasonable, belief does not come easily for you. You must "go against the grain" of years to achieve the blessed state of being "as a little child." But *that*, My child, is where believing and receiving can meet—to your good and My glory.

February Eighth

For the gate is narrow and the way is hard, that leads to life, and those who find it are few.

Matthew 7:14

The King's highway is a narrow way. It is no smooth and painless path—it is the way the King Himself traveled when He tented among you for a season. Yes, the King's highway is the way of the cross.

The cross means death to that which would destroy life. Counterfeit paths lure many into places of peril and destruction. Like sheep they nibble their way out of the safety zone I have provided—and suffer loss and grief.

Remember this word, My child: The cross destroys that which would destroy life. The deaths that you experience on this highway are not worth comparing with the life I am constantly offering and providing in their stead.

February Ninth

Trust in the Lord for ever, for the Lord God is an everlasting rock.

Isaiah 26:4

As you move through the day, be mindful of Me. Listen in your heart for that "still, small voice." Let Me check your impulsive and cruel reactions to others. Become aware that you *are* hurtful and hateful when your pride is hurt. Let Me be your inner Companion and Guard against this side of you. I have only plans for good, so do not expect evil from Me—you do not need to defend yourself or your ideas.

February Tenth

My shield is with God, who saves the upright in heart.

Psalm 7:10

Go calmly into this day. Light arises in the darkness for the upright. My light is upon you, child, and I am near. Fear not what lies ahead. Calm your troubled mind with My peace. You are Mine, and My face is toward you for good. Let that assurance be your shield and buckler and your great reward.

February Eleventh

This is the day which the Lord has made; let us rejoice and be glad in it.
Psalm 118:24

Truly I tell you, you are Mine. I bought you with a great price: My own blood. You find it embarrassing to hear such tender words. This is what I meant when I told you that love means letting in. It is not your worthiness that is the issue. It is not to set you up in the wrong way. It is to heal the inner wounds and fill the inner emptiness that I speak to you in this way. Open your heart to Me, My son, and let us become acquainted with one another.

February Twelfth

The effect of righteousness will be peace.

Isaiah 32:17a

Your desire to avoid conflict is a part of the unreality you cling to. Your idea of a peaceful life is not My idea of it. You are not called to this false peace you mistakenly yearn for. You are called to the peace that passes understanding—peace amid the necessary clashes between light and darkness, truth and falsehood. When these clashes come, your duty is to seek to find the truth, hold the truth, uphold the truth and expose the falsehood. Many times you will lose the battle from the human point of view. But if you are being faithful to let the truth reign within, you will find the peace of which I am speaking.

February Thirteenth

The fear of man lays a snare, but he who trust in the Lord is safe.
Proverbs 29:25

I am never far from you, My child. My blessing is always at hand. When you feel separated from Me, no matter how dark and lonely it may seem, there is always a door into My presence.

I have claimed you for Myself, for purposes higher than you can dream. These are not to build up your natural pride, but to bring to fruition My creative purpose. Let go ambitions. Let go competitiveness. Let go jealousy that guards little hoards of supposed treasures of place and power. All this is rubble compared with the life I desire to impart to you and to others through you. I am never far from you, My child.

February Fourteenth

But I have trusted in Thy steadfast love; my heart shall rejoice in Thy salvation.

Psalm 13:5

Your thoughts are not My thoughts, says the Lord. My thoughts are thoughts of peace; your thoughts are full of turmoil and unease. It is not easy for you to abandon your thoughts in order to hear Mine. The patterns are deep and well worn. But they are rainless clouds that produce no harvest.

I invite you to learn of Me, My son. The way is still narrow and the gate is still strait that leads to life, and few there are who walk in it. Life is My gift to you. Life—life beyond mere existence—is My overflowing gift to you. Live it; do not despise nor deny it.

February Fifteenth

For My thoughts are not your thoughts, neither are your ways My ways, says the Lord.

Isaiah 55:8

Yes, My son, My mercies are beyond numbering and they *are* new every morning. It is My pleasure to do good things to My children and for My children. Just as you desire good for yours, I seek the good for Mine.

My ways are not your ways—and thereby you often become confused. You think of Me as one like yourself—but My love is a pure love—not contaminated with self and sin and guilt as is yours. So, as My love and My ever-new mercies operate in your life and the life of your loved ones, learn to *entrust* them *and* yourself to My tender care. Only then can you know the peace "that passes understanding"—for your peace will not depend on your understanding.

February Sixteenth

God exalted Him at His right hand as Leader and Savior, to give repentance and forgiveness of sins.

Acts 5:31

My son, the pain through which you are passing is a necessary part of the healing it is My purpose to effect. Turn your thoughts more to Me and away from the painful situation which grieves you. My mercies are sure and My promises are true. Remember what you have been told over and over—it is on ruins that I build. Therefore anything of the old state that is not yet ruined must be allowed to crumble.

I want you to let go two things: a demand to be justified in relation to the past, and a willingness to go into condemnation when confronted with accusation. Take responsibility for bad judgment, for self-righteousness, for idolatry that sought to "carve" the idol to your liking. But having repented of these sins, accept My forgiveness and do not accept the accuser's wiles to destroy your faith and hope in Me. I am still God—and I still love everyone in this situation. You can count on that and you will find strength in it. Don't fight bitterness with bitterness.

February Seventeenth

Be still and know that I am God.

Psalm 46:10a

Yes, My son, I have heard your prayer, and I am speaking to you by My Spirit. Take heed and listen to what the Spirit says. You are reaching a dangerous part of the road you travel. There will be many distractions and temptations. But I will be with you to steady you on your course. Only beware of the subtle snares the enemy will set in your path. They will cause much pain if you allow yourself to be caught in them.

February Eighteenth

For the Lord loves justice; He will not forsake His saints.

Psalm 37:28

Yes, My son, I am your hope—your only hope—for this life and that which lies ahead. This is good news, for your hope in Me is secure. I do not abandon My people. As the Psalmist recorded, "Neither will He forsake His inheritance."

February Nineteenth

But if it is by grace, it is no longer on the basis of works; otherwise grace would no longer be grace.

Romans 11:6

My word is ever new, and it carries in it the power of renewal for your spirit. It is not given only for the moment it comes to you, but is a gift of My mercy to sustain and refresh you on your journey. At the right time, you may share these words with others, but do not be hasty about it. You will be given ample guidance as to when and how. Be careful not to allow this experience to puff you up in your own eyes and mind, but be humbled in your heart and know more deeply that it is all grace.

February Twentieth

Just so, I tell you, there will be more joy in heaven over one sinner who repents than over ninety-nine righteous persons who need no repentance.

Luke 15:7

You wonder many things and you wander over many areas of your past. It is like walking through a burned-over battleground. Here you are reminded of your sins and the inner pain of your former years—and you wander amid the ruins—a stranger still.

Yet through all the confusion and uncertainties of your growing years, I never left you nor abandoned you. The spark of fire, the touch of My love and yes, a Godly fear—did not depart. So here, before you leave these environs, bow your heart and give thanks for My sovereign grace. Give thanks that I have redeemed you and called you by name.

Give yourself freely now, My child, to the work I have set before you and to the people I have given you. Vain regret is not repentance. Repentance is a living, dynamic embrace of My ongoing will and purpose. *That* is the sacrifice which gladdens My heart, for it is the path of life for you.

February Twenty-first

But concerning love of the brethren you have no need to have any one write to you, for you yourselves have been taught by God to love one another.

I Thessalonians 4:9

My son, out of your depths you called upon Me, and I answered you. I have brought you through the dark valley and into this place and time of light. Know of a surety that it is I and not another who has done this. I want you to be so grounded in My faithfulness that you can share it with others. The inner knowledge you have gained through your recent trials gives added strength to your words to others who are facing dark times in their lives.

February Twenty-second

He who speaks on his own authority seeks his own glory; but he who seeks the glory of him who sent him is true.

John 7:18

My son, I do love you. Your fears and worries are needless luggage you carry on your trip through life. I would that you let Me take them from you, that your freedom might be a testimony to others. Bring them to Me, My child, and let Me deal with them. They are too much for you.

February Twenty-third

I have loved you with an everlasting love.

Jeremiah 31:3b

It is a good thing, My son, to give thanks for the multitude of blessings you have been given. Thankfulness is a healthy emotion—quite the opposite of the judgmental thoughts and feelings you entertain. Learn to give thanks for *all* things, not just the ones that bring pleasure. You will learn that I bring only good. Any cursing that comes is the result of your bad choices. So let thanksgiving "lead the way." It is the path to life, health, and wholeness.

February Twenty-fourth

But he who hears [My words] and does not do them is like a man who built a house on the ground without a foundation; against which the stream broke, and immediately it fell, and the ruin of that house was great.

Luke 6:49

I the Lord, am holy. I the Lord call you, My son, to greater holiness—holiness of thought, holiness of purpose. I am fashioning a people who bear the marks of My nature, who will be My witness in the present age, and will be with Me in the ages to come. I call you to be one of these—but your part is to struggle against the unholiness in your nature and to put on the nature I am offering you by My Spirit. Think on this today.

February Twenty-fifth

But he who is united to the Lord becomes one spirit with Him.

I Corinthians 6:17

Now, My son, hear My word to you today. Your battle is not done. There are still trials you must face. Keep yourself close to Me so that when the need is great, you will not be afraid. Remember that I love you and am with you in it all. And it *is* working together for your good. No success or failure compares with the gift of My sovereign love. Treasure it and you will find hidden strength for your needs.

February Twenty-sixth

For this slight momentary affliction is preparing for us an eternal weight of glory beyond all comparison.

II Corinthians 4:17

My mercy never runs out. It is an outflowing of My nature. I remind you of it often because your nature imposes a false idea of Me upon your heart. I am the Good Shepherd, and I seek only the good and welfare of My flock. Believe this, My son, and relax in My goodness. Fear has torment and love casts away both.

February Twenty-seventh

For God sent the Son into the world, not to condemn the world, but that the world might be saved through Him.

John 3:17

To you, My son, I have granted the grace to seek and hear My voice. You have chosen the "better part" which shall not be taken from you. Much darkness remains, but "light riseth in the darkness for the upright." You are seeking—and finding—light in your darkness. Pride still goes before a fall—and your pride is still a large source of your darkness. I require your willing cooperation in dealing a death blow to it, and you still draw back, misunderstanding My intention and My heart. O foolish one! How could you doubt that My plans for you are good and not evil? How could you go on cringing as from a hard master?

February Twenty-eighth

Despise not the chastening of the Almighty.

Job 5:17b

Listen and hear the echoes of eternity—the sounds of praise that only the just may hear. Listen with your heart, My son, and not just with your ears. You need the antidote to the negative thoughts and craven fear that you too often entertain. Be open!

February Twenty-ninth

All things were made through Him, and without Him was not anything made that was made.

John 1:3

The past is past, and I have covered it with the mantle of My mercy. Vain regrets and remembered failures can only lead to a dead end if you do not accept My all-encompassing forgiveness. It is pride that keeps the pain alive in remembering how you failed people and left hurt in your wake. Rather, watch the present where the same patterns are alive in you, and be diligent in avoiding the same sins under a different guise.

MARCH

Sing, my soul, His wondrous love,
    Who from yon bright throne above,
Ever watchful o'er our race,
    Still to man extends His grace.

Heaven and earth by Him were made;
    All is by His scepter swayed;
What are we that He should show
    So much love to us below?

God, the merciful and good,
    Bought us with the Savior's blood;
And, to make our safety sure,
    Guides us by His Spirit pure.

Sing, my soul, adore His Name!
    Let His glory be thy theme:
Praise Him till He calls thee home,
    Trust His love for all to come.

Anonymous, 1800

March First

If anyone is in Christ, he is a new creation; the old has passed away, behold, the new has come..

                                                        II Corinthians 5:17

Eternal peace abides in My presence. Know that here is rest from turmoil and a cure for the restlessness of your heart. Seek this peace more frequently, My son, for in it lies My healing, My wisdom, and My strength.

March Second

No one comprehends the thoughts of God except the Spirit of God.

                                                        I Corinthians 2:11b

I open and none can shut. I shut and none can open.

There are secrets and mysteries I have kept to Myself. They are to remain beyond the grasp and curious inquiry of man. They are part of the distance between creature and Creator. Beginning in the Garden, mankind has attempted to delve beyond its proper sphere. The tower of Babel is another occasion when My will overrode human ambition. I shut and none can open. But My action is always in keeping with My nature—My merciful care for My creation. It is not capricious nor arbitrary. I respect what I have made. Even in its fallen state, your nature still bears the imprint of My image, and My purpose is to bring that image back to its intended condition. Your pilgrimage, My son, is My path toward that goal. Open and shut doors are simply a part of that process, and it is all done in mercy.

March Third

My soul melts away for sorrow; strengthen me according to Thy word!
Psalm 119:28

I will strengthen you, help you and cause you to stand, upheld by My righteous, omnipotent Hand. That is My word to you today.

March Fourth

My grace is sufficient for you, for My power is made perfect in weakness.
II Corinthians 12:9

I am here. I have come according to My promised answer to your prayer. I am acquainted with all your ways and your thoughts, the desires and longings of your heart. I am the Merciful One and do not despise your feeble prayers.

Continue to look expectantly rather than fearfully to the future. On the one hand you maintain a positive and hopeful outlook, but personally you carry dark forebodings and groundless fears.

Remember, My son, it is the prayer of *faith* that moves mountains.

Enter into this mystery more fully, and *prove* Me, that I am able to do more abundantly than you ask or think.

March Fifth

When we cry, "Abba! Father!" it is the Spirit Himself bearing witness with our spirit that we are children of God, and if children, then heirs, heirs of God and fellow heirs with Christ.

Romans 8:15-16

Do not be afraid to write the words that come to you. Boldness in hearing and heeding is not presumption. I will check you at the proper time, and I do look for a freer, readier response to My voice, not only here in the quiet place, but throughout the day—hear and heed. Keep attuned to My world, and you will find an easier passage through yours.

March Sixth

Is My hand shortened, that it cannot redeem? Or have I no power to deliver?

Isaiah 50:2b

In the beauty of the morning My light dispels the shadows of night. In like manner My Spirit, the light of the world, dispels the shadows of your inner darkness. Where I dwell there is light.

Your doubts are doors into that darkness. Your questions are latches that open the doors into the gloom. Questions that cannot and will not be answered in this life lead to doubt and even to despair. But you can choose to set them aside and remain in the light of faith and trust. You can *choose* to walk by faith instead of insisting on walking by the sight of reason and answers to unanswerable questions. It is a humbler road, but one on which I journey with those who choose it. Be one of them, My son.

March Seventh

Praise the Lord! Praise the Lord, O my soul! I will praise the Lord as long as I live; I will sing praises to my God while I have being.

Psalm 146:1-2

It is My will to speak to you in your inner ear. Open, My son, to My voice. You do not make it happen, but you *can* prevent it, by filling your mind with vain thoughts.

The path before you is a good path. The shadows in the valley through which you have come are meant to *urge* you to seek the light—the light of My truth and My mercy. Do not carry the shadows with you as you emerge into this next chapter of your life. My sunlight radiates and drives out the doubts and fears. *Let, allow, permit* My goodness to dominate your soul. Work at it, My son, for your sake and for the fulfilling of My will through you.

March Eighth

Thou dost show me the path of life; in Thy presence there is fullness of joy, in Thy right hand are pleasures for evermore.

Psalm 16:11

There is no fear in love. There is no love in fear. I want you to recognize the basic element in the fears you entertain. Yes, you are embarrassed by the fear that gets exposed to others. Yes, you have repented of your fears, but I am calling you to go beyond that—and to do battle with your sinful nature. It is so deeply ingrained in you that it will take your repeated encounters to make progress here. Don't be put off by this, and don't give up. You have the weapons you need. Use them, and with them, expect My divine assistance. In this way, you *can* grow in love, the love that casts out fear.

March Ninth

Cast your burden on the Lord, and He will sustain you; He will never permit the righteous to be moved.

Psalm 55:22

Choose life! Choose thoughts and hopes of *life!* And turn away from the accusing fears that arise in your mind. I am calling you to *life*—to the abundance of life that you have not yet tasted. O My child, I am a generous and loving Father, and it is My pleasure to give abundantly. *Choose* to accept My proffered gift and *live*.

March Tenth

My sheep hear My voice, and I know them, and they follow Me.
John 10:27

Hearing and seeing inwardly are My gifts to My loved ones. Yet they must be cultivated and developed to become the full blessing I intend them to be. In the past you have often judged others who did indeed hear and see what was hidden from you. Your judgment put new blinders and stoppers on your own inner eyes and ears. When I give sight to the blind and hearing to the deaf, I am signaling *you* to allow this miracle to happen. You have no idea how much injury you have done with your faithless judgments. Be on guard, My son, when they rise up in you.

March Eleventh

It is these who follow the Lamb wherever He goes; these have been redeemed from mankind as first fruits for God and the Lamb.
Revelation 14:4

Mine it is to speak or be silent. Yours it is to wait and to listen. Ours it is to meet here, Spirit to spirit, and to renew our pledges of love. Mine it is to have mercy on you, and yours it is to remain aware that you are in constant need of this. Only in this way can your mind align itself with My will, and your steps be kept on the right path.

There is no shortage of mercy, no holding back on My part. It is My joy to have My children to receive and to rejoice in it.

March Twelfth

And the son said to him, "Father, I have sinned against heaven and before you; I am no longer worthy to be called your son." But the father said, . . . "Let us eat and make merry; for this my son was dead, and is alive again; he was lost, and is found."

Luke 15:21-24

Listening is hard for you, because you have always had many thoughts of your own. Or so you supposed, not knowing how to discern those that came from Me. Each day you come to Me with much doubt and inner restraint. It is as though you come with your ears stuffed with cotton, and only slowly take it away that you might begin to hear Me. I have told you that I am not reluctant to speak to you. It is your reluctance to hear that causes the long delay. Notice that when the "cotton is out," My words come through without delay.

My son, you are still in doubt of My love and care for you. You are still in the "slave" position—acting in fear and hiding. I invite you *home*, My child. You have always craved a home—and I tell you, of a truth, your true home is with Me. Nothing else will satisfy that inner yearning. Come home, and *quickly* begin to accept My divine, fatherly care. Live as a son and not as a slave!

March Thirteenth

Steadfast love and faithfulness will meet; righteousness and peace will kiss each other.

Psalm 85:10

I, the Lord, change not. In Me is no fickleness, no capricious judgment. My will is always, and in every case, right and true. This is the sure foundation for your own perception of right and wrong—My unchangeable truth and judgment. Mercy does not rule out judgment—"Mercy and truth have kissed each other." Because of this, judgment is to be feared only as it requires the loss of wrong and the choice of what is right. Sometimes this is painful and requires much struggle in the soul—a kind of birth-pang towards life.

There are structures of justice in your soul, but they are still mixed with the darkness of accusations against My mercy and goodness. Whenever these dark thoughts and feelings arise, you must make the hard choice of believing that My process is a merciful and loving one, even when circumstances *appear* otherwise.

March Fourteenth

Therefore come out from them, and be separate from them, says the Lord, and touch nothing unclean; then I will welcome you, and I will be a Father to you, and you shall be My sons and daughters, says the Lord Almighty.

II Corinthians 6:17-18

I have heard your prayer and your desire for more conscious dialog between us. You hold the key to this—and if you are willing to follow on, it shall be so.

Marvel not that I, the Lord of Heaven and Earth, leave this matter in your hands and heart. It is an expression of the dignity I have bestowed on My created sons and daughters. I have yielded to your key decisions in our relationship, so that the relationship may be based on grace and free choice. Only choices freely made can open the door to the goal I have in mind for you.

Another thing: do not worry so much about getting it all right. Of course you will make mistakes. You are hard of hearing, aren't you? But My love for you is great enough to protect you from serious errors or misinterpretation. Children stumble and fall as they learn to walk, and after all, My child, you aren't writing the Bible!

March Fifteenth

To you it has been given to know the secrets of the kingdom of God; but for others they are in parables, so that seeing they may not see, and hearing they may not understand.

Luke 8:10

It is My will for you to continue writing and speaking of My love. Others may give account of other aspects of My Word, but I want you to continue to sound a clear note on this theme. Most of your readers and hearers have only a slight realization of the depth of My love for them, and few, very few, allow the mystery to amaze them. There is a whole new experience in store for those who catch the vision and obey its beckoning light. I *want* to bless My children. Tell them of My love.

March Sixteenth

Every one who asks receives, and he who seeks finds, and to him who knocks it will be opened.

Matthew 7:8

Recognizing and welcoming My voice is essential if you are to continue in this new way. You still have a strong and over-riding mind which presents problems in following through with the path I have set before you. Take seriously, My son, your need to fight the distractions, for they rob you of much. Yes, you hear My voice, but you are still at the kindergarten level in this, so don't think more highly of yourself than you ought to think.

March Seventeenth

Lord, I am not worthy to have You come under my roof; but only say the word, and my servant will be healed.

Matthew 8:8b

This is a time of healing. It is a time for the repairing of breaches. Some of them have already begun to be repaired. Wholeness waits for My restoring grace. Marvel not that it is so, for I the Lord have promised and I fulfill My word. Be keenly aware of My leadings, for you will find some of them strange. But it will work out to bless you and others if you will simply trust Me and obey these leadings as best you know how.

March Eighteenth

Another of the disciples said to Him, "Lord, let me first go and bury my father." But Jesus said to him, "Follow Me, and leave the dead to bury their own dead."

Matthew 8:21-22

You do well to be thankful, My son, for thankfulness unlocks the door to greater mercies. Thankfulness unlocks the door of *your* heart so that you may recognize and welcome the mercies I have for you. Thankfulness dispels fear. Remember that! Your fears can be conquered if you will practice giving thanks. Concentrate on the *reasons* you have to be thankful when fear presents the uncertainties of what *might* be. You do well to be thankful!

March Nineteenth

Jesus looking upon him loved him, and said to him, "You lack one thing; go, sell what you have, and give to the poor, and you will have treasure in heaven; and come, follow Me." At that saying his countenance fell, and he went away sorrowful; for he had great possessions.

Mark 10:21-22

My child, do not close your ears and your mind to My voice out of fear of what I shall say to you! Have I not shown you My mercy at all times? There is no "unhappy surprise" awaiting you in what I shall say. My desire for you is to outgrow the underlying fear and nameless dread which has plagued you all your life. Your sins are forgiven—all of them—by My shed blood on the Cross. There is no condemnation awaiting you, even though you will need to confess and repent of any sin I convict you of. I say to you what I said in the Gospel again and again: Your sins are forgiven! It is not My will that you linger in morbid concentration on your wrongness. Rather, My heart is gladdened by your thanksgiving, praise and joy—*and* by your confidence in My eternal goodness. Keep listening for My word and plant yourself more surely on the Firm Foundation.

March Twentieth

If you then, who are evil, know how to give good gifts to your children, how much more will your Father who is in heaven give good things to those who ask Him.

Matthew 7:11

The images of your children are etched deeply in your memory. How much more are Mine etched on My heart! My wrath and My mercy are one—and both are meant to turn people to the saving path I place before them. Perfect, mature love casts out fear. When the heart is secure in Me, there is no ground for fear of My wrath.

Learning the height and depth of My love for you is a lifelong process. You have not chosen Me, but I have chosen you, and ordained you that you should bring forth much fruit. You will not see much of that fruit in this life, but My eye is upon it, and My will is carried forward through it. Marvel not at this. "By feeblest agents" does My righteous will get accomplished. Let My will bless you, My son, and take heart.

March Twenty-first

Day and night they never cease to sing, "Holy, holy, holy, is the Lord God Almighty, who was and is and is to come!"

Revelation 4:8b-9

Abiding in Me is the key to peace. Your heart can know no peace when you wander into the world. I am abiding in you, as I have promised. That is a reality—even though you are seldom aware of it. It you would "practice the presence" you would know greater peace and freedom, for I am here. Abiding in Me is your half of the equation. Blessings can and will multiply when you make that choice. It is the key to peace.

March Twenty-second

"They have no wine." And Jesus said to her, "O woman, what have you to do with Me? My hour has not yet come."

John 2:3b-4

My promises are not in vain. You have ample proof of this, My son, in the answers to your prayers. I want you to *exercise* your faith in My word. I want you to leave behind the caution and hesitation which are expressions of doubt. Move along the path I have laid out for you, and I will help you claim new ground. My promises are not in vain.

March Twenty-third

Today, when you hear His voice, do not harden your hearts.

Hebrews 4:7b

The unfolding of My plans takes place day by day. As day replaces night with the coming of the light, so does My light dispel the darkness in your soul. There is still much darkness there, My child, and I require your active cooperation in dispelling it. You can hide from the light of the sun and make a night even during the day. And you can hold back from My light if you choose. Watch for the temptation to this, and resist with My help—so that you move more steadily toward the fullness of day.

March Twenty-fourth

And the peace of God, which passes all understanding, will keep your hearts and your minds in Christ Jesus.

Philippians 4:7

You are My beloved child. You have been born again by My Spirit, grafted into the stock of Israel, made a member of My Body. This is your heritage, My gift of love to you. I have called you to make My Word known. You will never know all those you reach, and that is your protection against pride and vanity. It is enough to know you reach a few and bring a blessing to them. Be content, My child, with your lot. It is My gift of love to you.

March Twenty-fifth

And my God will supply every need of yours according to His riches in glory in Christ Jesus.

Philippians 4:19

My wisdom is not of this world. It seems foolish to the mind of the natural man. Yet I continually prove its value to those who find it. You still have too much reliance on human wisdom and too little trust in Mine. You are still too cautious in relinquishing *everything* to Me. I will do you no harm; I am your Savior, not your destroyer!

March Twenty-sixth

The Lord reproves him whom He loves, as a father the son in whom he delights.

Proverbs 3:12

I have a word for you. Can you accept it? Will you receive it? Good. Here it is: Judge not the situation by human standards. I am doing a special work—an important work that will advance My holy purpose and design here. It is all right. All is well. Please do not be afraid now. My love is stronger than the forces set against you. Remember that it is not you but Me who is their enemy. My strength is made manifest in your weakness. But do, My child, trust Me. Trust Me now while the outcome is still hidden from your eyes.

March Twenty-seventh

My son, if your heart is wise, my heart too will be glad.

Proverbs 23:15

Wandering about and lingering in doubt, you wait and hesitate. I, too, wait to be gracious. I do not delay in coming to you. The delay is yours, My son. The enemy is ever ready to seek an entrance into your thoughts—interfering with our appointed meeting. The loss is yours, for I am ready to lead you into a more stable and productive relationship. I am not playing spiritual games with you. I rebuke you,

My son, for your lack of willingness to fight harder against this torpor and uncommitted attitude.

Come to Me expecting to be spoken to like a man. Come to Me expecting to speak your need, but not to wallow in it.

March Twenty-eighth

The peace of God, it is no peace,
  But strife closed in the sod.
Yet, brothers, pray for but one thing—
  The marvelous peace of God.
                    W.A. Percy, 1924

I have called you and ordained you for My own purposes. You do not and cannot know all My plans or provisions. You can see how, like Elijah, you and your family were provided for, how the road opened up before you in unexpected ways, leading you far from where you began your journey. These things are not "accidents"— they are manifestations of My sovereign grace operating behind the scenes of your outward life. As I unfold them to you, I want you to record them as a testimony to Me. Faith is rooted in such soil, and you can extend the blessing if you are obedient. I will show you further how to carry this out. Be at peace.

March Twenty-ninth

And great crowds came to Him, bringing with them the lame, the maimed, the blind, the dumb, and many others, and they put them at His feet; and He healed them.

Matthew 15:30

My son, do not forget "the pit from which you were digged, nor the rock from which you were hewn," the humble beginning of your life. There was and is a purpose and design through it all, and that is still to be fully realized. Be attentive to My leading in this matter, so that My full intent may be realized.

The angel of My mercy has followed you all the days of your life. My protection has covered you and shielded you from many dangers. Your "forty years" wandering in the desert of your own choosing has reaped sorrow for you and others. But My loving kindness has not departed from you, and My hand is still upon you. My glory is still seen in broken vessels.

March Thirtieth

From the rising of the sun to its setting the name of the Lord is to be praised!

Psalm 113:3

It is good to wait in My presence. You are being blessed and fed by My Spirit, even when you hear no words. It is good to keep trusting when your prayers are delayed. You have been long in coming to this place, and there is still much ground to reclaim. You have built a fortress around your mind, and trusted in your own thoughts and opinions rather than in Me. They failed you when great need arose, and you were faced with your inability to help. I have not failed you, but you forfeited much peace by your choices. It is good to wait in My presence. This too is part of My work to help you regain and reclaim lost ground.

March Thirty-first

Wait for the Lord, and keep to His way, and He will exalt you to possess the land.

Psalm 37:34

Wait, My son, wait. My purposes are yet hidden from your understanding. In spite of all I have said to you, you still do not grasp the vision I have for you. Your impulsive tendency to lurch ahead can cause problems that do not need to arise. That is why I counsel, "Wait!"

APRIL

O for a closer walk with God,
    A calm and heavenly frame,
A light to shine upon the road
    That leads me to the Lamb!

Return, O holy Dove, return,
    Sweet messenger of rest!
I hate the sins that made Thee mourn
    And drove Thee from my breast.

The dearest idol I have known,
    Whate'er that idol be,
Help me to tear it from Thy throne,
    And worship only Thee.

So shall my walk be close with God,
    Calm and serene my frame;
So purer light shall mark the road
    That leads me to the Lamb.

William Cowper, 1772

April First

I am the resurrection and the life; he who believes in Me, though he die, yet shall he live, and whoever lives and believes in Me shall never die.

John 11:25-26

This is My word for you today: Take heed to everything I say— not just in this morning hour, but throughout the day. I will guide you and help you, My son, if you will keep a listening ear. You cannot chart the day without Me, and you are not strong enough to stand against your adversaries without Me. Do not overestimate your strength nor underestimate that of the enemy. You have ample evidence to show what a weak pawn you are in his hand when you separate yourself from My loving care. So do not be a foolish son who despises his father's instruction, but be wise in your weakness, and keep listening to Me.

April Second

Draw near to God and He will draw near to you.

James 4:8

Call upon Me, and I will answer you. Draw near to Me and I will draw near to you. This is ever My word and My promise. I know your frame and your weakness. I know the difficulty you have in staying your thoughts on Me. I know all about you—more, much more than you know about yourself. So come to Me in your brokenness, your failure to measure up, your craven, baseless fears. I will not turn you away, because I love you. You will come to know Me as I reveal My love to you. Call upon Me and I *will* answer you.

April Third

One thing have I asked of the Lord, that will I seek after; that I may dwell in the house of the Lord all the days of my life, to behold the beauty of the Lord, and to inquire in His temple.

Psalm 27:4

Beauty for ashes. Life for death. Cleansing for sin. Joy for sorrow. These, My son, are My rate of exchange. These are the necessary funds you bring in our commerce. "Thou hast received gifts for men: yea, for the rebellious also, that the Lord God might dwell among them" (Psalm 68:18).

Your mind does not perceive nor comprehend this divine exchange, but your spirit knows and rejoices. You have nought to bring but these products of your old nature, but I turn them to beauty, to joy, to hope. See and behold, My child, how blessed are those who trust in Me.

April Fourth

I am the light of the world; he that follows Me will not walk in darkness, but will have the light of life.

John 8:12

According to your faith be it unto you, O you of little faith! Your lack of faith leaves your soul shriveled and bent—for a whole dimension is under-developed. Your reasoning and doubt is over-developed. And the distortion hinders your walk with Me. I have given you ample reason to trust Me with your whole heart. I have given you more than you ask or thought. So the time is here for faith to flourish and catch up—will you allow it to happen?

April Fifth

For those whom He foreknew He also predestined to be conformed to the image of His Son.

Romans 8:29a

The spirit of prayer is My gift to you. It is the means by which you open the doors of your heart, the gates of your soul, to Me. I will come into that guarded place only when you open the gate to Me. So when the holy Spirit moves you to open the gates, do so heartily and expectantly.

A little child, seeking its mother's breast, is not distracted easily.

Its hunger drives it to a single-mindedness and a concentration that you will do well to emulate. Here at the throne of grace there is nourishment, refreshment, and guidance for your daily needs. I do not want you to miss the riches of grace, the showers of blessing, I have prepared for you.

April Sixth

I believe I shall see the goodness of the Lord in the land of the living!
Psalm 27:13

My son, I bid you be of good cheer. Your floundering and uneasy state is not necessary. There is a place of rest. There is a place of settled peace. Lean harder on My breast. Gather your thoughts like wayward sheep and enfold them in Me. My ample bosom has room for all. My mercy covers you even though you do not feel or sense it. I still wait for you to exercise greater trust in Me. "Cast out the bondwoman." Cast out that which binds you to your old faithless thoughts and fears. Be of good cheer in My presence, for that is a sign of your trust and the fruit of it.

April Seventh

You are not your own; you were bought with a price. So glorify God in your body.

I Corinthians 6:19b-20

Pray to Me, My son, pray to Me. You are still prayerless through much of your day. You still have not learned the secret of continual fellowship with Me, and you walk through much of your day cut off, as it were, from Me. I am still with you, but your life would be much more fruitful if you learned the secret of praying without ceasing. It is an attitude—not an activity. It is possible even in busy hours to maintain the spirit of prayer. I have told you to turn every circumstance and care into prayer. I repeat My words. Turn *everything* into prayer—thanksgiving or petition, praise or intercession. Practice! Repent of your past passivity and spiritual torpor! Awake to the possibilities I hold before you, and engage in this struggle. Signs still follow those who follow My word.

April Eighth

Unless a grain of wheat falls into the earth and dies, it remains alone; but if it dies, it bears much fruit.

John 12:24

The race is not to the swift, nor the battle to the strong. The weak and wounded can still fight and *win*. Courage is but trust in My unfailing help. It is the by-product and fruit of staying with Me. I am the Lord of battle—and it is My desire to see you overcome the cowardice and faithlessness you have nourished. You cannot save yourself; you cannot give yourself life. But these gifts you already have. Cherish them, My son, and know that what I have given is ample ground on which to stand when doubts and fears assail your soul.

April Ninth

Let your light so shine before men, that they may see your good works and give glory to your Father who is in heaven.

Matthew 5:16

The light on your path never goes out. It is always enough to guide you along the chosen way. If your way seems dark and uncertain, find out where you have willfully chosen another path. My way is not always easy—but it is always good.

I have compassion on you and your family. Much suffering has been experienced in all of you. I know your case and My work is not yet complete. My glory shall yet be revealed, so do not lose heart!

April Tenth

I will sing to the Lord as long as I live; I will sing praise to my God while I have being.

Psalm 104:33

Go in peace to the day's journey. Walk with Me in your heart. Be attentive to the still, small voice within to check you when you would leave the path that I have chosen. Believe, My child, and trust My presence. Do not allow the adversary to lure you into his way of thinking and feeling. Let My will be your desire and you will have a blessed day.

April Eleventh

But they who wait for the Lord shall renew their strength.

Isaiah 40:31a

The clamor of this world has dulled your ears to the sound of My voice. I still speak as to Elijah in the "still, small voice." As long as your heart is pulled after worldly delights, the dullness will persist. Only as and if you center more and more on My will and My concerns will you find it easy to hear.

I counsel you once again, do not lose heart. Do not forget that "they who wait on the Lord shall renew their strength." And they also will improve their hearing as well.

April Twelfth

He that goes forth weeping, bearing the seed for sowing, shall come home with shouts of joy, bringing his sheaves with him.

Psalm 126:6

These are new days for you, My child, they are days of harvesting—of reaping and ripening. Do not doubt that they are from Me and the fruit of My mercy. My kindness shall not depart from you. That is My sovereign and solemn promise. All My dealings with you are mercy.

Do not be ashamed of your weakness and need. They are the material with which I work to bless you and others through you—and in this, I am glorified. Only remember to return to the Giver the sacrifice of a thankful heart.

April Thirteenth

He can deal gently with the ignorant and wayward, since he himself is beset with weakness.

Hebrews 5:2

Today I am leading you along a path you have not walked before. To your eye, it may seem familiar and ordinary. But you have not lived "here" before—for each new moment is just that: new. Do not allow the ordinariness of the day to obscure its true reality, My child.

April Fourteenth

As obedient children, do not be conformed to the passions of your former ignorance.

I Peter 1:14

My dear child, walking in obedience is done a step at a time. It is not yours to seek the long view, for you would then be tempted to seize the control of your path, thinking you knew the way. I am the Way and by the simple act of obeying step by step, you will arrive at the goal. Build up your own faith in this way, and encourage other fainthearted souls to do the same. Strong faith comes from pressing on when the outcome seems uncertain.

April Fifteenth

We are children of God, and if children, then heirs, heirs of God and fellow heirs with Christ.

Romans 8:16b-17a

My purpose in all My dealings with you is one: to bring you to Me. The pain and the joy have the same intent on My part. If you will look at it in this light, My child, you will find it easier to walk through the hard times. I have no pleasure in seeing My children in pain—except the joy of seeing them triumph over it in faith. This is the victory that overcomes: the faith-knowledge that you are still being led home—to Me. Be of good cheer.

April Sixteenth

Therefore I tell you, whatever you ask in prayer, believe that you receive it, and you will.

Mark 11:24

In the book of remembrance, write: "Hitherto the Lord has helped me." In the book of remembrance, recall My acts of mercy. Let the memory of past mercies cheer you in hard places. As I have been faithful of old, I will not cease to be faithful now. Your way is laid out before you. My plan unfolds day by day. Hitherto I have helped you, and today I am the same.

April Seventeenth

What I tell you in the dark, utter in the light; and what you hear whispered, proclaim upon the housetops.

Matthew 10:27

Your lack of faith and courage to move at My word is a great handicap in your servanthood. I have bidden you to be bold in listening for My voice and heeding My word. Unless you learn to put aside the murmurings of unbelief, you will quench the precious gift of My Spirit's voice. Think you that I have brought you this far to confound you and allow you to veer off in strange paths?

April Eighteenth

Everyone to whom much is given, of him will much be required.

Luke 12:48b

You are My beloved child. I know you and see you with all your faults and sin. I have redeemed you. You are Mine. But I will not countenance your sin and rebellion against Me. That I will deal with in justice and mercy.

Do not withdraw from Me in pride and fear. Let My gracious words assure you that My love is greater than your sin, greater than your need. There is no shortage of grace and mercy as we walk together. Smile at your foes, for they will not prevail.

April Nineteenth

I dwell in the high and holy place, and also with him who is of a contrite and humble spirit, to revive the heart of the contrite.

Isaiah 57:15b

The broken and contrite heart is the work of My grace. Blessed are they who weep over their sin and shed tears of joy over My mercy. Blessed are they who find the secret place when we commune Spirit to spirit. Many are they who call on Me in distress, but few who yearn for such times of trysting. Guard well this privilege, My son. Never take it for granted or treat it as casual or ordinary. It is part of My preparatory work on your soul.

April Twentieth

Peace I leave with you; My peace I give to you; not as the world gives do I give to you.

John 14:27a

I will ordain peace for you, for I have wrought all your works within you (Isaiah 26).

My peace passes "understanding" because I give it in the midst of trouble. Perplexing circumstances are no barrier to My gift.

This is a season of peace—a time of renewal of spirit. Enter it with enthusiasm and claim it fully—for your sake and the sake of others. Fear and foreboding are sins against My mercy. Allow no place for them.

Do not mistake this for a vacation from conflict. My battle is not done, so to that end, keep alert to the enemy's stratagems. He cannot prevail if you keep your eyes and your heart stayed on Me. I am your safety, your fortress in the battle.

I want you to be a bringer of peace—a conveyer of My peace. That can only happen if you are "peace-full" yourself. So fill your cup—drink deeply at this "peace-well"—and all will be well.

April Twenty-first

Commune with your own hearts on your beds, and be silent!
Psalm 4:4b

Be still and know that I am God. Be still, for in the stillness you will come to know what you cannot learn in your impatient movement. How seldom you are ever quiet within! Even when you are doing nothing, there is still strain and tension, indicating an absence of the stillness. Stilling the murmurs, the dissatisfaction, the jealousies, the hurts, and the vain ambitions—these you can do with My proffered help. They will not go away without your active choice against them. Stillness will follow, but you must claim it by rejecting these roots of unrest in your soul. Be still and you will know.

April Twenty-second

Among those born of women there has risen no one greater than John the Baptist; yet he who is least in the kingdom of heaven is greater than he.

Matthew 11:11

Praise befits the upright. Praise befits the fallen. Praise befits those who have been forgiven and restored. This is your daily walk. Many times, My child, you fall back into your old ways of thinking and reacting. You are never far from this danger, and I am aware of it. My kind and fatherly hand is over you, else you would plunge headfirst into the pit. Keep coming back to Me as soon as you are aware of what is happening. I will help you. I will keep you—but you *must* choose to forsake your way for Mine. It is the only way.

April Twenty-third

But for me it is good to be near God.

Psalm 73:28a

Pride. Double-mindedness. Self-absorption. These block your hearing, My son. The pure in heart shall see Me. The single-minded ones hear Me. But when you have *any* mixture of motives, when you allow pride to rise up, and jealousy—your ears are stopped. I wait for you to recognize and repent—so that our fellowship can be reestablished.

I warn you, My son, not to take this privilege lightly. Others have foundered on these "sin rocks" and made shipwreck of their faith. The fear of the Lord is still the beginning of wisdom.

April Twenty-fourth

Search me, O God, and know my heart! Try me and know my thoughts! And see if there be any wicked way in me, and lead me in the way everlasting!

Psalm 139:23-24

Showers of blessing! It is My joy to shower blessings on My children. It is My joy to see a soul growing in My image and likeness. These things you cannot see clearly. But I tell you that such a process is going on and must go on. Look for the showers of blessing, My child. Pray for them, not only for yourself, but for those I have laid on your heart. Showers of blessing! Let your prayers "unlock" the heavens, that all may be blessed, and My joy may be completed in yours.

April Twenty-fifth

O Israel, if you would but listen to Me!

Psalm 81:8b

The walk of faith to which I call you is a walk from death to life. Out of the death of the old life, you are being led daily *into* life. It is an ongoing process, and there will be no end to it while you are on this earth. It is a journey, a life-pilgrimage—and each day you have new opportunities to go further along the way. Do not be surprised that you have no comfortable place to settle without conflict and challenge. That is not the condition of this journey—for the world, the flesh, and the devil still war for your soul. There *is* grace even in the midst of the necessary conflict—so seek that peace and go on with Me.

April Twenty-sixth

Make me to know Thy ways, O Lord; teach me Thy paths. Lead me in Thy truth and teach me.

Psalm 25:4-5a

The entrance of My word still gives light—it comes into the darkness of your mind and reveals to you what you could not see. I am not only the light of the world, I am the life-giving light of your soul. Yet My light brings pain. Your "soul-eyes" blink and turn away from what I reveal. Steady your eyes, My child, and accustom them to living in My light. The darkness may be more comfortable to the flesh, but only the light brings life—true life—everlasting life. Choose light and life and let the darkness pass.

April Twenty-seventh

And let the peace of Christ rule in your hearts, to which indeed you were called in the one body. And be thankful.

Colossians 3:15

I have told you before to expect no great revelations, and not to despise the simple ones I give you. This is your protection, My son, against the part of your nature that would grasp such revelations and take pride in them. This "lower" level is a safe one for you, and feeds the soul true nourishment. Remember, My son, that I dwell with those of a humble and contrite heart. Seek *that* heart, and we shall abide together in harmony.

April Twenty-eighth

I am a man under authority, with soldiers under me; and I say to one, "Go," and he goes, and to another, "Come," and he comes, and to my slave, "Do this," and he does it.

Matthew 8:9

I want you to learn to move boldly and quickly when I speak to you. You are beset by many misgivings and doubts, and these hinder your growth in Me. Those who would walk with Me must learn this secret, for it transfers the "control" out of your hands. I know the fears that come into your mind, but I tell you this: Your hesitation and reasoning are more harmful than any mistake you would make in obeying what you believe to be My will. Avoiding one error, you fall into a greater one. Learn, My son, that I am not playing games with you.

April Twenty-ninth

I have heard your prayer, I have seen your tears; . . . I will deliver you and this city, . . . and defend this city.

Isaiah 38:5b-6

It is no accident that things are working out as they are. Although many minds and separate decisions are involved, I am still able to move My will and My plans forward. "I plant My footsteps in the sea and ride upon the storm." Marvel if you must, My child, but do not allow blindness to hinder My divine and sovereign hand. Bring your prayers to Me with the fullness of faith that I am able to do exceedingly, abundantly above that you ask or think. Be a believer, My son—and be a witness to My faithfulness.

April Thirtieth

And your ears shall hear a word behind you, saying, "This is the way, walk in it," when you turn to the right or when you turn to the left.
Isaiah 30:21

Yes, I have heard your cry, and you are hearing My voice. Depart not from it to the left nor to the right. Depend on My fatherly protection and providence. Desire more of Me and less of the tainted treasure of the world. Direct your thoughts to Me at all times, for therein is your peace. Doubts come easily to you, My child, because you have indulged and entertained them so frequently. They do not need to have dominion over you, for I am with you to strengthen your feeble faith and invigorate your hope. Yes, I have heard your cry, and you are hearing My voice. Be of good cheer.

MAY

I sought the Lord, and afterward I knew
    He moved my soul to seek Him, seeking me;
It was not I that found, O Savior true;
    No, I was found of Thee.

Thou didst reach forth Thy hand and mine enfold;
    I walked and sank not on the storm-vexed sea;
'Twas not so much that I on Thee took hold
    As Thou, dear Lord, on me.

I find, I walk, I love, but O the whole
    Of love is but my answer, Lord, to Thee!
For Thou wast long beforehand with my soul;
    Always Thou lovedst me.

Anon., c. 1904

May First

For now we see in a mirror dimly, but then face to face. Now I know in part; then I shall understand fully, even as I have been fully understood.
I Corinthians 13:12

Think, My son, of the miracle of life. It will strengthen you in the time of trial. Into an earthly frame of dust I have breathed My Spirit. The dust is still dust, but every cell is animated with *life*. This is a *sharing* on My part. Life does not belong to this earth—life is My gift. You marvel at its many forms. Some are beautiful to your eyes, others are grotesque. Some are repulsive, but all share in this miracle of life. Reflect on it, for you can grow more faith-filled if you allow the miraculous gift to fill you with wonder and gratitude.

May Second

The Lord is my shepherd, I shall not want.
Psalm 23:1

By flowing streams I lead My flock. They shall not be left in the desert of desire. My living water I supply, that in their thirst they shall not die. Be refreshed at the river of life, My child, and know it ever flows from My throne. Your thirst can never be slaked elsewhere, but here and here alone. Cleansing, too, these waters offer, so stop, and wash, and drink, and live.

May Third

The friendship of the Lord is for those who fear Him, and He makes known to them His covenant.

Psalm 25:14

Be still! Be still, My child. Let anxious thoughts subside, and old accusing ones die. I am the One who brought you safe thus far—I am the One who over-ruled the raging seas of your ambitions and emotions. I am the One who steered you into a safe haven. Be still! Rejoice! Rejoice at the remembrance of My holiness. Rejoice at the remembrance of My deliverances. Rejoice that you are known and loved.

Repent! Let the conviction of My Holy Spirit move you to abandon the strongholds of sin in your heart. Let My light penetrate the places of deception and falsehood—that the truth may free you more and more to live in harmony with Me.

May Fourth

. . . Jesus the pioneer and perfecter of our faith, who for the joy that was set before Him endured the cross, despising the shame, and is seated at the right hand of the throne of God.

Hebrews 12:2

You have found a way to use these words for the betterment of your soul. Continue to meditate on them and let their truth penetrate more deeply into your heart. The fruit they bear will be a blessing to you and a joy to My heart. You still have far, far to go to realize how much I love and care for you—and for "all who have loved My appearing." This world with its violent and bloody rebellion against Me and against itself, is held together by the prayers, praise, and faithfulness of the remnant who listen and heed My voice.

May Fifth

No good thing does the Lord withhold from those who walk uprightly. O Lord of hosts, blessed is the man who trusts in Thee!

Psalm 84:11b-12

My ear is always open to the cry of My children. None calls to Me in vain. Your cries and prayers are heard and laid up—deposited in My heart—and I will not forget them. I have committed Myself to be a prayer-hearer. You have come late to the place of prayer.

Although you learned early that I answer prayer, you did not grow in true prayer. For you it was a cry in a tight spot. It is meant to be more—much more than a cry for help in desperation. Yet even that I do not despise, because I know it *can* lead on beyond itself. True prayer still takes place in the secret place where we can commune as Friend with friend. Treasure it, My son, and grow in it.

May Sixth

Beloved, do not believe every spirit, but test the spirits to see whether they are of God. . . . By this you know the Spirit of God: every spirit which confesses that Jesus Christ has come in the flesh is of God.

I John 4:1, 2

You do well to fear self-deception in listening for My voice, for without a healthy fear there is no "testing of the spirits." Your own mind has been in control for so long that you did not know or recognize when your thoughts were not your own. My thoughts are often unrecognized and unheeded—to your loss.

My thoughts are not your thoughts and frequently contradict yours. It is very important that you practice this listening, so that you can be led beyond the scope of your narrow and limited vision. Self cannot be allowed to control—for self is always interested in immediate satisfaction and gratification. My ways are not your ways. The breaking, the pain, the denial of your short-term wishes and goals are all contained in My larger view of your good and blessing. I cannot fail you—only *you* can fail you.

May Seventh

I blessed the Most High, and praised and honored Him who lives for ever.
Daniel 4:34b

Keep praising! Praise brings light into your darkness and health into your sickness. Keep praising! You are blessed even as you bless. You are built up even as you remember and extol My works. My joy is fulfilled in your joy. My will is fulfilled in the harmony between your spirit and My Spirit. That harmony is the music of the spheres. That harmony is the echo of My creative plan. You but touch its edges, but even that is not to be despised. Keep praising. There are mysteries here that you have not begun to plumb.

May Eighth

Paul said, "Whether short or long, I would to God that not only you but also all who hear me this day might become such as I am—except for these chains."

Acts 26:29

This is My word to you today: Forget yourself and let your heart go out to others. Seek to put My will ahead of yours, and all will be well.

May Ninth

The true light that enlightens every man was coming into the world.

John 1:9

This is My word today: Let your eye of faith see through and beyond the clouds of doubt and guilt. My light is constant, and there is no variableness nor shadow of change in Me. Receive My light as it comes through whatever channel or servant. Keep on seeking *light* and the shadows *will* flee away.

May Tenth

He showed me . . . on either side of the river, the tree of life with its twelve kinds of fruit, yielding its fruit each month.

Revelation 22:1-2a

The tree of life yields its fruit in season. The cross blossoms with new beauty when you come to Me with your repentance. Far deeper than you can know, I plant the seed of My word in you. Hidden from your eyes, the growth *is* taking place. Your despair and your depression are merely the products of your unbelief. Put away sorrow, put away anxiety, put away the hurt and jealousy you feel—and *rejoice* that the tree *will* bear its fruit in season. Have I not told you?

May Eleventh

Catch us the foxes, the little foxes, that spoil the vineyards.

Song of Solomon 2:15

Rejoice in the gifts I give you, My child, but rejoice more and more in Me. I am the source of true joy, the antidote for sadness that clings to your soul. Joy and sadness meet together as you repent and find My forgiveness.

Watch the "little foxes"—the destroyers of peace and harmony. Watch more carefully their coming before they do their destructive work. I will help you, but you must put forth your effort to *choose* against them.

May Twelfth

Those who are well have no need of a physician, but those who are sick.
Matthew 9:12b

My mercy extends to the lowest and the basest. Those who are high or great in their own sight cannot receive or appropriate it. They are cut off from grace by their own choices.

As you come to see how much self reigns in you, bring your sorrow, your penitence and conviction to Me. You can do that much; I will deal with the rest according to My sovereign will and wisdom. Just keep bringing *self* to Me.

May Thirteenth

But I trust in Thee, O Lord, I say, "Thou art my God." My times are in Thy hand.

Psalm 31:14-15a

I will lead you and guide you with the "little thoughts" that come into your mind—*if* you will obey them. Test the spirits, but do not fear to follow My leading. Remember, My child, that I am your protector and that I watch over My word. If you are to "will one thing" as you say you want to, you must learn to obey more faithfully these leadings of My Spirit.

May Fourteenth

Fret not yourself; it tends only to evil.

Psalm 37:8b

Do not fret yourself about situations you cannot change. It is part of your acceptance of your weakness and impotence in situations that are beyond your control. You have good words for others. Apply them to yourself and *focus* on the responsibilities I have laid on you. In your obedience to these you will be blessed and you will be a blessing. Do not waste yourself in fretting.

May Fifteenth

Thou whose glory above the heavens is chanted by the mouth of babes and infants.

Psalm 8:1b-2a

You know more than you know you know. My Spirit has revealed to your spirit knowledge beyond words. It is, in a very real sense, a secret knowledge, because the world neither knows nor can know it. I have chosen to keep back from curious eyes and doubting minds what I have revealed to "babes and sucklings." Treasure the glimpse I give you of this gift. It is greater than you think!

May Sixteenth

I believe that I shall see the goodness of the Lord in the land of the living!
Psalm 27:13

It is not for you to fathom the mysteries of My kingdom, My child. It is for you to enter into them by faith. Your "rational," reasoning, questioning mind has put many barriers in your way. You remain "outside" the mystery, looking in—or even looking away—rather than entering through the open door. Remember, child, that I rent the temple veil from top to bottom—that the likes of you might come into the holy of holies. I want to see you get beyond where you are and taste the goodness of the Lord as you have not done.

May Seventeenth

For He has made known to us in all wisdom and insight the mystery of His will, according to His purpose which He set forth in Christ.
Ephesians 1:9

Life! I have called you to life. The shadows of death linger too long in your thoughts. Live *today* the life I am giving you. Put away *your* vain and wicked fears about tomorrow! For freedom I have made you free and for life I have given you life. It's here for you, My child, if you will take it. "Lay hold on life and it shall be your joy and crown eternally."

May Eighteenth

Take delight in the Lord, and He will give you the desires of your heart.
Psalm 37:4

Delight yourself in Me, My son, and know that such delight is your true inheritance. My joy and My peace are gifts I delight to share. The world is a sad place. There is much suffering, pain and sorrow. Yet there is also, intermingled with it, a joy to be found. My purpose is still unfolding, and there are many evidences of it to those with eyes to see. So there is good reason to "delight yourself in Me."

May Nineteenth

My times are in Thy hand; deliver me from the hand of my enemies and persecutors!
Psalm 31:15

Be assured that I am watching over you and yours. Be at peace about their present conditions and locations. I know where they are and how to deal with them. Your task is to trust and entrust them in My keeping.

May Twentieth

He said to them, "It is not for you to know times or seasons which the Father has fixed by His own authority."

Acts 1:7

Verily I say to you, My son, it is enough that you hear and receive these simple words of encouragement and assurance. The boundaries of our mind and experience are such that there will always be things too hard for you to understand. Your demand to know must be replaced by a desire to love, to obey, to please Me. That is the real path to blessing and fulfillment. The "knowledge path" is never going to fill your deepest needs. Re-think, and be more diligent to find what I have for you.

May Twenty-first

The Lord is my light and my salvation; whom shall I fear?

Psalm 27:1

Bright and glorious is the light of My presence. Dark and gloomy is your heart when you depart from Me. Choose to stay in My light, My child, and let the darkness flee from you. You are called to be a child of the light.

May Twenty-second

Return, every one from his evil way, and amend your ways and your doings.

Jeremiah 18:11b

Remember what I have told you, My son: Repentance is not regret. It is not remorse over sins remembered. It is *change*. It is a decisive step away from the past into the light of My grace and love. Yes, remorse and regret will remain, for the memory of the break in fellowship with Me can serve as an added stimulant to resist temptation when it comes. Foolish one! Do not think that drawing near to Me will cause temptation to cease. The trials will come, but there is abundant grace waiting for you each time I call you to go through the valley.

May Twenty-third

Let them curse, but do Thou bless! Let my assailants be put to shame; may Thy servant be glad!

Psalm 109:28

Bless those who curse you. Bless and curse not. It is not for you to condemn another soul, no matter how far into darkness it has sunk. That is My concern, and I call you to a different task. By consciously blessing your enemies, you become a part of an assault of light against the darkness of this world. There is great need for the assault, for the darkness is great and growing.

Rejoice, My child, at the daily gifts My love brings into your life. Again I say to you, rejoice! Let the beauty and love that you see and experience today outweigh and dispel any negative, faithless thoughts.

May Twenty-fourth

I have loved you with an everlasting love; therefore I have continued My faithfulness to you

Jeremiah 31:3b

You can only love Me more as you love yourself less. These two loves are in conflict and competition with one another. The love you have for yourself is fraught with anxiety and impossible demands. It is a cruel love, not a freeing one. When you allow My love to take possession of your heart, these cruel demands and fears fall away. There is no *need* for self-love because My love fills all. It is the paradox of paradoxes. All is won as all is lost.

May Twenty-fifth

If you keep My commandments, you will abide in My love, just as I have kept My Father's commandments and abide in His love.

John 15:10

No child of Mine is "ordinary." Each one is precious—not the product of mass production. Of course you must be warned against thinking too highly of yourself, because your tendency is to go from the depths of self-hate and rejection to the height of self-love and congratulation. My love for you is a steady, unchanging love that is not based on your uniqueness nor your worthiness. It is hard for you to grasp the reality of it, but My Spirit has brought the reality of it to you. You can abide in My love because My love is here for you to abide in. I want you to remember this today. I am here, and I love you.

May Twenty-sixth

I the Lord make Myself known to him in a vision, I speak with him in a dream.

Numbers 12:6b

I give to My beloved in sleep. In the unconscious I often speak— dark and strange words to your waking mind. But the spirit knows, recognizes and receives. So be at peace, My child, and do not doubt that My gifts are still abundant. Take heart and be ready to exercise the gift I have given you freely. It is My pleasure to give good gifts to My children.

May Twenty-seventh

Jesus Christ is the same yesterday and today and for ever.
Hebrews 13:8

My dear child, I have not changed, I am still the same—yesterday, today and forever. I counsel you to ground your soul in this truth. Clouds may temporarily hide the sun but they do not *change* the sun. So with My love for you. Clouds may hide it for a time, but I do not change and My love is ever toward you and with you. Rest in the reality of it.

May Twenty-eighth

I became a minister according to the divine office which was given to me for you, to make the word of God fully known, the mystery hidden for ages and generations but now made manifest to His saints.

Colossians 1:25-26

When I tell you to lift up your heart, I am giving you the opportunity to come out of your enclosed, fear-ridden world into My world. When you lift your heart to Me, I open Mine to you. Remember that, so the words will not be perfunctory, rote sounds, but a real choice on your part.

You are but at the threshold of the mystery Paul talked about in Colossians. You have eschewed mystery and have sought to reduce all mysteries to your understanding. What folly! Your limited mind can touch "the hem of My garment" but can *never* plumb the mystery of My love.

Lift up your heart to Me, My child, and *expect* that I will open My heart to you.

May Twenty-ninth

For a day in Thy courts is better than a thousand elsewhere.
Psalm 84:10a

My goodness never fails, My child. This is a day of My goodness. Let it unfold its blessings and let My love carry you through.

May Thirtieth

O that My people would listen to Me, that Israel would walk in My ways!
Psalm 81:13

Trust My words more implicitly. Give up your time and energy-wasting reasoning. Be willing, My child, to be foolish in the eyes of others in order to be wise in My sight. Remember that the world around you still walks in darkness, even though the light has come. Its reasoning and wisdom are folly. Do not be seduced by them.

Trust My words more implicitly and walk with Me.

May Thirty-first

I will hope continually, and will praise Thee yet more and more.
Psalm 71:14

This is My word today: Anxiety has no place in our relationship. Your anxiety is rooted in lack of faith in My overarching, prevailing goodness. I have given assurances and have fulfilled promises. Let your eyes focus on *that* reality and turn away from vain imaginations. This is a time for *faith*. Believe as you have never believed before—*let* yourself believe and not hold back!

JUNE

This is my Father's world,
    And to my listening ears,
All nature sings, and round me
    Rings the music of the spheres.
This is my Father's world:
    I rest me in the thought
Of rocks and trees, of skies and seas;
    His hands the wonder wrought.

This is my Father's world,
    The birds their carols raise,
The morning light, the lily white,
    Declare their Maker's praise.
This is my Father's world:
    He shines in all that's fair;
In the rustling grass I hear Him pass,
    He speaks to me everywhere.

This is my Father's world,
    O let me ne'er forget
That though the wrong seems oft so strong,
    God is the Ruler yet.
This is my Father's world:
    The battle is not done;
Jesus who died shall be satisfied,
    And earth and heaven be one.

Maltbie D. Babcock, 1901

June First

For the gifts and the call of God are irrevocable.

Romans 11:29

I call whom I will to be with Me. This does not make them special in any way; it is the expression of My sovereign will. You have always balked at this truth, My child, and even now your mind scrambles for explanations and exceptions. Far better for you simply to accept the reality inasmuch as you can, and leave the unfolding to Me. There is mystery here, and you have always wanted everything to be crystal clear. It cannot be so, for I am God and you are clay. It is enough for you to know that I love you and am watching over you. Go about your duties in *that* light and be content.

June Second

Do not be anxious beforehand what you are to say; but say whatever is given you in that hour.

Mark 13:11

I communicate with you, My child, in many different ways. Sometimes a thought is given, full blown, as it were, and it is yours to act on, to accept or reject. Sometimes My communication is wordless silence—a "sense" of My mercy and love. However it comes, I want you to become more aware and sensitive to the *living* reality that I am with you and that the "lines" are open. You do not call Me in vain, nor speak to an empty space. Remember that, believe it, practice it.

June Third

For the word of God is living and active, sharper than any two-edged sword, piercing to the division of soul and spirit, of joints and marrow, and discerning the thoughts and intentions of the heart.

Hebrews 4:12

Yes, there is a discerning between soul and spirit—the dividing of joint and marrow, the sword of My Spirit. You receive My word in your spirit by My Spirit. It is My word, not yours. You are free to interpret it and speak it, but I want you always to remember that it is from Me. Because of your lack of faith, you have difficulty fully trusting and acting on the words I speak to you. You still keep your eye on "those" whom you value, whose opinions and reactions to you are more important than your obedience to Me. I have been very patient with you, for I know your frame and remember who you are. But unless you overcome this fault, you will *never* fulfill the task for which I have prepared you.

June Fourth

O Lord, I pray Thee, open his eyes that he may see.

II Kings 6:17a

The sun! Remember the sun is always shining, even when clouds are thickest. Much of your life is spent with more attention to the clouds than the sun. This is a serious flaw and hindrance in our relationship, because you are, in effect, denying the sun's overarching reality. I am the light of the world, My child, and the light still shines. Choose light rather than clouds today!

June Fifth

Who are you to pass judgment on the servant of another?

Romans 14:4a

It is not for you to know all the intimate details of controversies past and present. This feeds something in you that is not good. You raise yourself "above" those who are on the wrong side according to your light. Beware the subtle attraction to this, My child, and see the danger it poses for you. You must choose a more narrow path, and give up judging others who are wrong. Keep your life and your mind more focused on your tasks. Do not drain away your energies by this fruitless habit.

June Sixth

While they were talking and discussing together, Jesus Himself drew near and went with them. But their eyes were kept from recognizing Him.

Luke 24:15-16

I will be with you, communicating My word to you through this day. Keep your ears and heart open, so that My word will bear the fruitful harvest for which I send it. Walk with Me, My child—and learn to be more aware of My presence in your life.

June Seventh

Behold, I am with you and will keep you wherever you go, and will bring you back to this land; for I will not leave you until I have done that of which I have spoken to you.

Genesis 28:15

Go into this day assured of My sovereign, eternal love. Let no cloud of doubt hide My reality from you. You are a child of clay— mortal, vulnerable to temptation, able to depart from Me. But you are mine, and you are held in My hand. Doubt it not, My child, but lift up your head and press on.

June Eighth

Cast your burden on the Lord, and He will sustain you; He will never permit the righteous to be moved.

Psalm 55:22

As you begin to write what I am saying to you, My word flows more freely into your mind. Your great hesitation in starting is frustrating to you and need not be. It is time to trust more and more quickly, because you should know by now that I will not fail you nor let you down. You have much to learn in this process, and learning involves the willingness to go on past the safe places. So do not hesitate to begin, even in your "unsureness." Give over to Me the role of protecting and guarding My word!

June Ninth

Then you shall take delight in the Lord, and I will make you ride upon the heights of the earth; I will feed you with the heritage of Jacob your father, for the mouth of the Lord has spoken.

Isaiah 58:14

My word is still a lamp for your feet and a light for your path. My word is hidden in the words you read, and in those that come to you. I am the living God, and speak living words to My people. Much is lost because your own hearing blots out My voice. Your life would be more productive and fuller if you would learn to listen more and talk less. Watch especially the barbed tongue, My child.

June Tenth

Lot's wife looked back, and she became a pillar of salt.

Genesis 19:26

Move ahead on this path. Do not linger over past memories and failures. They are gone, but if you dwell on them, they will keep you from present obedience. My mercy, not your goodness, is your hope. The time is now for you to reclaim the lost years and enter into the harvest years. Move ahead on this path. Redeem the time—and enjoy it.

June Eleventh

Jesus looked up and said to her, "Woman, where are they? Has no one condemned you?" She said, "No one, Lord." And Jesus said, "Neither do I condemn you; go, and do not sin again."

John 8:10-11

Open your heart to receive My word, and open your mouth to speak it. Open your arms to receive and return My love through others. Your way is known, your path is secure. "No evil shall befall you, neither shall any plague come nigh thy dwelling."

It is not necessary to dwell in the shame and condemnation that old memories bring up. Let them drive you quickly to Me, My child, and let Me assure you that My blood cleanses from *all* sin. Leave behind what is behind and set your face forward to the future I am giving you day by day. Steady your thoughts on Me and let go the shame and condemnation.

June Twelfth

But I have trusted in Thy steadfast love; my heart shall rejoice in Thy salvation. I will sing to the Lord, because He has dealt bountifully with me.

Psalm 13:5-6

It is enough that you know My mercies toward you in the past. Stand on that solid ground when you feel afraid. You have every reason to trust that I will sustain and keep you to the end. Do not let the vain thoughts and fears that come to you remain—cast them out in My strong name. You have a solid ground on which to stand and fight the battle of faith!

June Thirteenth

His master said to him, "Well done, . . . enter into the joy of your master."
Matthew 25:21

The spirit of heaviness still covers your heart. My Spirit is light and peace. Why do you dwell in darkness, My son, when My light is shining? Not your feelings—but the *reality* of My love and power. Give over your way, your burden, and let the light penetrate the dark places.

This *must* be a day of rejoicing. My loving kindness has overflowed upon you and redeemed your life from destruction. Enter into the blessings I have prepared for you, and do not hold back! My Spirit is light and peace.

June Fourteenth

For the commandment is a lamp and the teaching a light, and the reproofs of discipline are the way of life.

Proverbs 6:23

Do not neglect these prayer and listening times. Things are not as "cut and dried" as you tend to think, and your participation in the process makes a difference. Your dull and listless prayers indicate a certain boredom with the routine, and signal a serious state of lukewarmness. Repent of your wayward nature and return to Me, My child, that we may go on together in your journey.

June Fifteenth

The Lord will be your everlasting light, and your God will be your glory.
Isaiah 60:19b

My glory is hidden from the world. My glory is revealed only to the souls who seek Me. It is not glory as the world understands it. Inasmuch as your heart still craves the glory of the world, you cannot see or experience Mine. Continue to fight your desire to win, to be vindicated, to be appreciated and recognized. They are blinders that keep you from the true glory. You have far to go—so be active in carrying on the struggle. I will help you, but the fight must be waged by you.

June Sixteenth

He leads the humble in what is right, and teaches the humble His way.
Psalm 25:9

Your overweening pride is an ever-present threat to your spiritual progress. I have sent you many blows against it, but it is still far from death. Under various disguises it lives and thrives. It will not die without pain. Yet the pain it causes for you and for others is greater. I have covered you with My protective hand to make possible the process needed with the least pain to you. You still do not realize how obnoxious and repulsive your pride is to Me and to others. If you could see it in that light, you might be more willing to let it go. O My son—do let it go!

June Seventeenth

When you pass through the waters I will be with you; and through the rivers, they shall not overwhelm you; when you walk through fire you shall not be burned, and the flame shall not consume you. You are precious in My eyes, and honored, and I love you.

Isaiah 43:2,4a

Go peacefully amid the cares of this day. Allow My peace to prevail over anxious or worried thoughts. Remember, My child, that the race is not to the swift, nor the battle to the strong. My way is still a hidden one from the natural eye, and only by faith can you behold the wonder and glory of it. But if you choose, you can behold—and be held in the way.

June Eighteenth

Do not forget the works of God; but keep His commandments so you should not be like your fathers, a stubborn and rebellious generation, a generation whose heart was not steadfast.

Psalm 78:7-8

Like trees planted by rivers of water, I plant the souls of My children in the deep soil of My love. Like trees planted in good soil I look for fruit, the product of life lived unto Me. Sink your roots deep into My love and bear good fruit.

June Nineteenth

My people . . . have forsaken Me, the fountain of living waters, and hewed out cisterns for themselves, broken cisterns, that can hold no water.

Jeremiah 2:13

My praise is a healing stream. It washes away the impurities that cling to the soul. Praise befits the upright. It harmonizes with the life lived before Me. Praise is not seemly with the heart set on its own path. Let My praise flood the dark corners, illuminate the unanswered questions, and bring hope into every moment of despair. My child, do not deprive yourself of this blessing!

June Twentieth

The Lord reigns; let the earth rejoice.

Psalm 97:1a

I have heard your prayers and the longing of your heart. I will not leave you nor forsake you, My child. The road ahead is clear and you have nothing to fear. Rejoice with Me in the way. The songs I have given My people are songs of rejoicing. They are more than a stirring of the emotions. They are the sounds of triumph over the enemy of your soul. Use them as weapons in the fight.

Be at peace with your neighbor—do not allow opinions to wound and separate you one from another. Be careful to fight on the right front, and do not be tricked into trying to win your point. This is important.

June Twenty-first

Let us conduct ourselves becomingly as in the day, not in . . . quarreling and jealousy.

Romans 13:13

How can you expect anything to come to a preoccupied mind? A double-minded man is unstable in all his ways. Your lack of concentration, of "recollection," is a fruit of your undisciplined mind. I have warned you before that you must fight against the fragmentation of thought and stay your mind on Me. I would gladly speak and commune with you, but your indulgence in your thoughts puts a barrier between us.

June Twenty-second

Everyone who is of the truth hears My voice.

John 18:37c

The quiet impressions that I bring to your mind are to be heeded and treasured. Do not wait for some overwhelming word, but learn to listen attentively to the still, small voice. I will protect and guard you from being led in wrong paths—only be courageous and dare to listen, hear and heed!

June Twenty-third

My heart stands in awe of Thy words. I rejoice at Thy word like one who finds great spoil. I hate and abhor falsehood, but I love Thy law.
Psalm 119:161b-163

"O Lord, send Thou prosperity." The prosperity I send is health of soul. It comes with poverty of spirit. It comes with a longing for more of Me. Prosperity is not fatness of carnality—the abundance of *things*. That is the world's view. But My child, seek true prosperity through the door of a broken and contrite heart. Not good feeling but true fellowship with My Spirit—that is the prosperity I send.

June Twenty-fourth

As a hart longs for flowing streams, so longs my soul for Thee, O God. My soul thirsts for God, for the living God.

Psalm 42:1,2a

The mountains! The mountains! Look away to the hills. My purposes and plans go far beyond your narrow horizon. The long view, the distant view, can help you overcome your intense self-absorption.

Today I call you to write these messages. Keep your thoughts focused in that direction. Don't waste time! Be about your Father's business. You are not here to play. The path will clear before you, but you must take the steps yourself.

June Twenty-fifth

Behold, Thou desirest truth in the inward being; therefore teach me wisdom in my secret heart.

Psalm 51:6

Do not fret yourself over the unfinished state of those you love. Trust Me that I am still at work and can make all things new. Truly I say to you, look up, wait, pray and believe, and you will see My glory. I am the true and faithful One, and My promises *never* fail.

June Twenty-sixth

Create in me a clean heart, O God, and put a new and right spirit within me. Cast me not away from Thy presence, and take not Thy holy Spirit from me. Restore to me the joy of Thy salvation, and uphold me with a willing spirit.

Psalm 51:10-12

It is enough that you wait for My word and continue to draw your mind away from its wanderings. I remember who and whose you are. And My mercy covers your feeble efforts. There are no spiritual heroics here—just your needy, broken spirit, and My all-sufficient Spirit of grace. I do not want you to become discouraged at what seems a lack of progress in these morning meetings. Yours is not an unusual case. Persevere, My son, persevere.

June Twenty-seventh

Peace I leave with you; My peace I give to you; not as the world gives do I give to you. Let not your hearts be troubled, neither let them be afraid.

John 14:27

I want My word to reach many hearts. My fatherly care extends to all My children, and many of them do not know Me. They are in need of truth and light. The entrance of My word gives light—so I send it into dark places. All I require of you is a willingness to be a channel of truth and hope. It is not a "great" ministry, but it is life-bringing to those who sit in the shadow of death. If you will keep this in mind, we can accomplish My will. Your blessings will be multiplied, and your reward will be more than you can know. So you have nothing to lose by your willingness to "be a fool" for My sake.

June Twenty-eighth

You will seek Me and find Me, when you seek Me with all your heart.

Jeremiah 29:13

This is a hard assignment for you, My child, one for which you were not ready in earlier years. Your "readiness" now is fragile, susceptible to temptation and failure. Disobedience is costly in this case. You are being entrusted with My words to go to many hearts. Only I can know the extent and use I will make of them. They are not given for you alone, as I have told you before—though I reassure you again that they *are* for you. I am making you a steward of them—"entrusting" them into your hand. Stay in a straight—and yes, strait—course, and all will be well.

June Twenty-ninth

I will run in the way of Thy commandments.

Psalm 119:32a

Commit your way—all the way—into My hand. Committing is letting go the control of your journey. It is allowing your own plans, dreams, hopes, and ambitions to be set aside in favor of My holy will. It is not so mysterious as it sounds, and it is not as obscure as you try to make it. Your problem is letting go—even the little hidden "strings" that stay attached after you have seemingly surrendered all. O child of My love, My way is the way of love and life—abundant life. It may appear restrictive to your warped vision, but in the process you will find that what I say is very truth. Step by step, just let go your way and choose Mine—by the light I give you. That is all.

June Thirtieth

The time is fulfilled, and the kingdom of God is at hand; repent, and believe in the gospel.

Mark 1:15

It is My pleasure to give good gifts to My children. I do not give according to their deserving, but as I see best. Sometimes I withhold gifts, because they would not bring a blessing with them. Material gifts are a special problem in this regard. They are easily turned into distractions and misuse. So I withhold them, waiting until the soul is ready and able to bear them. When the heart attaches itself to worldly goods or Mammon, the blessing is lost. Walk carefully now, My child, amid the myriad gifts I have bestowed. Don't let the gifts come between us.

JULY

Fairest Lord Jesus, Ruler of all nature,
  O Thou of God and man the Son,
Thee will I cherish, Thee will I honor,
  Thou, my soul's Glory, Joy, and Crown.

Fair are the meadows, Fairer still the woodlands,
  Robed in the blooming garb of spring:
Jesus is fairer, Jesus is purer,
  Who makes the woeful heart to sing.

Fair is the sunshine, Fairer still the moonlight,
  And all the twinkling, starry host:
Jesus shines brighter, Jesus shines purer,
  Than all the angels heaven can boast.

German, seventeenth century

July First

Let us then with confidence draw near to the throne of grace, that we may receive mercy and find grace to help in time of need.

Hebrews 4:16

Beside the still waters I bid you pause and rest. Soul-rest needs quietness—the stillness of My presence. Turbulence abounds when you seek your will, when you linger in old guilts and regrets, when you worry about your future or that of your loved ones. But if you will linger here, My child, and accept the quietness of spirit I offer you, you may go on your way rejoicing in hope. Frantic striving does not accomplish My perfect will, no matter how well-intentioned. "Whoso offereth praise glorifieth Me." So pause, praise, refresh your soul in My still waters, and be renewed.

July Second

Who are you to pass judgment on the servant of another?

Romans 14:4a

Leave those I have called to Myself to Me. Fret not about their present condition. Many things are still hidden from your view, and that is as it should be. Focus your eyes and your attention on the present. Keep faith with My faithfulness. Simplify your demands to know and understand, and be thankful for the light I am shining on your path. Clear the clutter that impedes your journey and hold your head upright as we move along—together.

July Third

Being ignorant of the righteousness that comes from God, and seeking to establish their own, they did not submit to God's righteousness.

Romans 10:3

This is My word for you today, My child: Put away falsehood and live in reality. Let go the vain imaginations that invade your thoughts with distracting frequency. Forge a weapon of prayer against these energy-draining intruders. Learn to recognize the ploy of your adversary.

My presence is with you, though you do not sense or realize it. It is not a palpable sensation to be sought but a reality to be recognized. I am fulfilling My promises and proceeding with My purpose. You do not need to be babied at this point, but to keep your mind and heart fixed on accomplishing My will for you.

July Fourth

They loved the praise of men more than the praise of God.

John 12:43

Learn to love the hidden life. You still look and long for approval and recognition. I ask you this: Do you want man's approval or Mine? Do you want to honor Me or to be honored? These are not idle questions. They go to the very heart of our relationship. I have poured out My love on you in many ways. Seeking and longing for recognition and praise is a form of spiritual adultery. Yes, it is *that* serious!

July Fifth

I will not look on you in anger, for I am merciful, says the Lord.

Jeremiah 3:12b

My heart of mercy is a never-failing source of supply. The stream of mercy never runs dry. Mercy is not given to evoke praise. It is an outflowing of My essence, My nature. Therefore My gifts are lavished on the just and the unjust, the grateful and the ungrateful. But only those whose hearts are set aflame with My love can be truly blest. They are those who choose to walk with Me. They are those who turn their faces toward My light and long with ardent desire to be lightened. Be one of those blest souls, My child. Let My mercy find its fulfillment in you.

July Sixth

Whenever you stand praying, forgive, if you have anything against any one; so that your Father also who is in heaven may forgive you your trespasses.

Mark 11:25

And now, My son, be at peace with yourself and with others. Let no grudge or hurt remain lodged in your heart. Remember My words, "Forgive as we forgive," and struggle against the desire to hold on to some injury from the past.

A free people is a forgiven people. A free soul is a forgiving soul. Where you hold back the forgiveness you keep yourself in bondage. There is much to learn about this miracle—the grace of forgiveness. And there is much need of it, both in your life and the life of others. Don't wait for them, but heed My word for yourself.

July Seventh

Take My yoke upon you, and learn from Me; for I am gentle and lowly in heart, and you will find rest for your souls. For My yoke is easy, and My burden is light.

Matthew 11:29-30

You are blocking out My voice with your anxious thoughts. You are not trusting Me to work in the situation for good. Self is at the center, not Jesus. You can repent and turn if you choose. Your burden is heavy, My child. My burden is light.

July Eighth

I am with you always, to the close of the age.

Matthew 28:20b

These things I have spoken to you to bring to your remembrance the basic realities of your life. At the center of all that comes to you, I am present—by will or by allowance—but you are never, *never* without Me. If you could grasp this with surety, how great a difference it could make in your experience. When I said to My disciples, "Lo, I am with you always, to the close of the age," I included you— your specific time and need—in that promise. This is the central, basic reality which can drive away the demons and shadows of the night.

July Ninth

Incline your ear, and come to Me; hear, that your soul may live; and I will make with you an everlasting covenant.

Isaiah 55:3

I come to you, My dear sheep, as a Shepherd caring for His own. I know your ways, and My watchful eye is ever on you. I guard the portal of your life, so that you are ever safe in My providence. Yet you must guard the portals of your own heart. I have given you the responsibility and privilege of keeping charge of your heart. Your carelessness there brings on needless suffering. Your faithlessness and laziness leave the door unguarded. Unlike real sheep, you stand on a higher level of dignity and duty. Only as you struggle toward a steadier and more faithful watch will you be freed from the painful consequence of your carelessness.

July Tenth

This was to show God's righteousness, because in His divine forbearance He had passed over former sins; it was to prove at the present time that He Himself is righteous and that He justifies him who has faith in Jesus.

Romans 3:25b-26

It is enough, My child, that you seek to love and obey according to the light I give you, not yours to unravel the mysteries of life. Be careful not to become hard and withdrawn when you are in the company of those whose thoughts and understandings differ from yours. Seek a placid and irenic spirit. In that you will be a blessing instead of a stumbling block. I will be with you to warn when danger approaches. Listen, heed, and obey—and reap the blessing.

July Eleventh

The Lord is my shepherd, I shall not want. He leads me beside still waters; He restores my soul.

Psalm 23:1a,2b,3a

With joy you shall draw water from the wells of salvation. The wells are deep and sometimes you must wait for the plumbing of the depths. The surface of your soul is like the surface of the sea—busily moving in many directions as the gusts of wind blow on it. There is a restlessness there that must be gotten past. Or change the picture,

My child, and compare it to a dry and thirsty desert—unstable and shifting in many directions. So do not be discouraged that I require you to go deeper than the shifting sand, the restless sea. Quietness is in the depths. The "water of salvation" is plentiful and pure, but must be *drawn* from its source. Since most of your life is lived on the surface, it is all the more necessary that you take the time to go deep and tap the life-giving wells.

July Twelfth

Come now, let us reason together, says the Lord: though your sins are like scarlet, they shall be as white as snow.

Isaiah 1:18a

Whiter than snow! That is the miracle of the forgiven soul. That is the miracle of My grace. I seek the sullied and soiled souls of My children, and wait to be gracious. I see the turmoil and pain, and wait to bestow the Balm of Gilead. I am afflicted in the afflictions of My children, but there is no cheap shortcut to alleviate their pain. I am God and not man. My universe moves according to My design and wisdom, and I uphold it according to My wisdom and power.

Yet I am moved to bring healing for hurt, and salvation for sinners. My love reaches out, stirs and troubles the wayward heart, that it might turn and live.

Whiter than snow! That is the miracle I desire to make possible by My grace.

July Thirteenth

Why do you stand here idle all day? Go into the vineyard too. I choose to give to this last as I give to you. The last will be first, and the first last.
                                    Matthew 20:6b,7b,14b,16

Take advantage of the opportunities I am giving you, My son, to bear a faithful witness to Me. Do not esteem them lightly. They are not accidental or coincidental. The years wasted in the past are gone. They cannot and need not be recalled. I am the Lord of years! The circumstances surrounding you now are *designed* to be a blessing, and to bring forth the harvest of your life. My strength and guidance will be supplied all along the way. You are to be a late laborer in the vineyard, so take advantage of all I have made possible. I have crowned the years with My goodness. Crown yours with faithfulness, My son.

July Fourteenth

How long will you go limping with two different opinions? If the Lord is God, follow Him.

I Kings 18:21b

Choose this day whom you will serve. Remember, the choice is always yours. The choice is "whom you will serve," not "will you serve?" For if you allow yourself the luxury of thinking you don't need to choose, you have already *made* a choice.

Do not be foolish, My child, and do not waste the time I am giving you to bring forth a fruitful harvest. The hour is already late, so you need to bear that in mind as you make your choice today.

July Fifteenth

People will not endure sound teaching, but having itching ears they will accumulate for themselves teachers to suit their own likings, and will turn away from listening to the truth and wander into myths.

II Timothy 4:3-4

Do not fret yourself about those whose ideas and opinions—and beliefs—differ from yours. Truth is truth, and I am the source of all true knowledge and understanding. Hold onto the light I have given you. Hold it in gratitude and humility. You did not create it nor earn it. It is My free gift of love. But you do not have *all* the light. There is much you neither know nor understand. That is the way it should be. Only do not fear and fret when others seem to know, or claim to know, something that is new, strange or even alien in your view of things. Draw near to Me, and let Me be all you desire or need. Humility is the key to peace here, My son. Not having to know. Just trusting and loving. . . .

July Sixteenth

This is My beloved Son, with whom I am well pleased; listen to Him.
Matthew 17:5b

The voice of the Father, the Son, and the Spirit is one voice. That is why you cannot distinguish between them in these daily conversations. Only your curiosity or vain imaginations would cause you to question My words.

You see little or no advancement in these quiet times. Looking back to what you heard, you see yourself still "stuck" with the same old problems now as you had then. Why does this surprise you, My child? Why do you expect to become other than what you are? Change and growth do not obliterate the old nature, the carnal heart still produces the same fruit. Forgiveness following heartfelt repentance is still the answer. Tears are the fertilizer to bring for hidden fruit. So My word today is, "Keep on."

July Seventeenth

He will not break a bruised reed or quench a smoldering wick, till He brings justice to victory.

Matthew 12:20

You are a broken reed and smoldering flax. As far as worldly ambition and goals are concerned, you are a failure. Your former dreams turned sour, even bitter, and only very gradually have you come to grips with the full meaning of your loss. I have dealt a hard and severe blow to your pride, and yet you have managed to rehabilitate it and prop it up. Self-deception is at the root of this, and you can only make yourself more ridiculous by clinging to the flotsam and jetsam of your shipwreck. Remember, My child, that it was for your greater good that I allowed the death of dreams. My path is a path of life, a path of burdens, a path of hope. But pride cannot walk the path without stumbling. Let Me free you of this unnecessary burden—and show you even yet that My mercy is better than your dreams.

July Eighteenth

From the rising of the sun to its setting the name of the Lord is to be praised!

Psalm 113:3

In the brightness of the morning, My glory shines. In the darkness of the evening, My mystery remains. There it is, My child—as long as you sojourn here, you will acquaint yourself with My glory and My mysteries. Your soul grows both in the revealed and that which remains hidden from your understanding. Bless and praise Me in both, for it is all working for your eternal joy. Remember, child, that My love is eternal.

July Nineteenth

Nevertheless, not as I will, but as Thou wilt.

Matthew 26:39c

You are being tested on many fronts in the circumstances of your life. Each day I offer you a way through these perplexities and give you the privilege of making good choices. This is My grace at work. You are not a robot, programmed to behave in a certain way. I have created and redeemed you to give you this inestimable privilege. Keep alert to what I am saying, My son, so that with the test you will also see and choose My proffered way through. Set negative feelings aside and press on toward the goal.

July Twentieth

Goodness and mercy shall follow me all the days of my life; and I shall dwell in the house of the Lord for ever.

Psalm 23:6

It is time again to cast all your cares and burdens on Me. There is a way to carry your responsibilities lightly but not carelessly. It is found here at My mercy seat, My throne of grace. If you will bring these cares and burdens to Me and *trust* Me to help you, you can go out in peace and carry out your part. That is My plan and My wish for you and all My loved ones. It is not a passive, presumptuous attitude I am asking of you, but a loving, trusting expectancy that grace will abound and the way will appear. Faith is walking and working in this expectancy.

July Twenty-first

As it is, I rejoice, not because you were grieved, but because you were grieved into repenting. For godly grief produces a repentance that leads to salvation and brings no regret, but worldly grief produces death.

II Corinthians 7:9a-10

You cannot see the work I am doing in your soul, My child. It must remain hidden from your eyes. There is no cause for despair or pride. The work is Mine, the outcome is Mine. Yours is the task I have set before you. Keep on the path I have laid out for you. Watch the little foxes that destroy the vine—the easy carelessness, drifting back into old patterns of thought and words. I am still doing a new thing, My child, so keep trusting that "the old has passed, behold, the new is here." I am your daily "newness" and refreshment.

July Twenty-second

The God of our fathers appointed you to know His will, to see the Just One and to hear a voice from His mouth; for you will be a witness for Him to all men of what you have seen and heard.

Acts 22:14-15

You are a chosen vessel of My mercy. Just as you choose instruments and vessels in your ordinary course of life, I choose souls with whom and through whom I intend to accomplish some part of My plan. No honor accrues to the "chosen" but, unlike the instruments you use, Mine require cooperation. It is not a preprogrammed thing. So do not flinch at My choice, and do not waste time in doubting it. Get your eyes off *you*, and look up where mercy reigns and where My will is to shower blessing beyond your farthest thought.

July Twenty-third

Rejoice in so far as you share Christ's sufferings, that you may also rejoice and be glad when His glory is revealed. If you are reproached for the name of Christ, you are blessed, because the spirit of glory and of God rests upon you.

I Peter 4:13-14

Not in the height of elation is true joy to be found, My son, but in the quiet places of the heart. Too much "happiness" tends to make you giddy and unwise. A more somber scene is safer for you.

Yet I know your longing for "joy unspeakable and full of glory." I know how hard it is for you to allow gladness to drive away shadows of doubt and fear. So I bid you, child, to draw near to My heart. Do not worry about details of feelings, and avoid introspection about your motives. I will attend to all that. I want you to be a child of the upward look. I want you to seek My face, My merciful visage in all the circumstances of your day. This will take concentration and focus—because it is so new to you. But *do* try!

July Twenty-fourth

Do not fear the people of the land, for they are bread for us; their protection is removed from them, and the Lord is with us; do not fear them.
                                                              Numbers 14:9

I have given you this thought that you might explore the idea with your brethren. There are many ways of expressing and conveying the life/truth I am imparting to you. Do not be afraid to venture out with new thoughts.

The Grapes of Eschol are symbolic of the enormity of My provision and the limitless possibilities I have planted in your future. Only the craven fear and faithless forgetfulness of what I have already done can hold you back. Joshua and Caleb had the vision to go forward, but the nay-saying spirit prevailed and the people suffered. Let the largeness of My mercy carry you across the barriers of the path—and go forward into the Promised Land.

July Twenty-fifth

Thy word is a lamp to my feet and a light to my path. I have sworn an oath and confirmed it, to observe Thy righteous ordinances.

Psalm 119:105-106

It is My pleasure to give good gifts to My children—and the gift of My word is My choicest gift. You must learn to treasure it more deeply, My son, for it is not to be despised. Grieve not My Spirit by taking a casual attitude toward the gift I am giving you.

Truly I say to you, do not think the journey is over and the day is done. Do not seek to be released from My yoke and burden. At the right time, you may lay it down, but not before. I will provide the necessary strength and health. Make no mistake about that. Redeem these days—they are harvest days.

July Twenty-sixth

I have loved you with an everlasting love; therefore I have continued My faithfulness to you.

Jeremiah 31:3b

Drink deeply at the fountain of My love. Do not be content with quick sips in your hurry to be on your way. Thirsty souls are renewed and refreshed if they will take the time and trouble to drink deeply. These are the waters of comfort—the springs of strength for the day's journey.

Sometimes the waters of comfort are bitter. They do not please the natural man. Sometimes they contain purging agents to purify—and must be taken in if they are to serve their wholesome purpose. When I say, "drink deeply at the fountain of My love," I want you to understand that bitter or sweet, the water of life is the fountain of love. It can be no other, My child, for God is love.

July Twenty-seventh

Open your mouth wide, and I will fill it.

Psalm 81:10b

Write this: I have long put My word in your mouth. You have not known, indeed you cannot know the purpose and object to which I sent it. It is not your word—it is Mine. Be faithful in speaking what I give you. The glory shall not be yours, but Mine. Multiply the occasions to praise Me by being faithful in what I set before you. Faithfulness brings forth praise.

July Twenty-eighth

For if you forgive men their trespasses, your heavenly Father also will forgive you; but if you do not forgive men their trespasses, neither will your Father forgive your trespasses.

Matthew 6:14-15

See how great a fire a little word kindles! See how great a storm surges when one contrary breeze blows! Such is your vanity, My son, that you allow small things to be magnified and treated as great matters. You rob yourself of peace and grieve My Spirit by your persistence in this old pattern.

Do you love Me more than these? Do you *want* My presence more than the tawdry toys you feel you have lost? Wake up, child! You cannot play with your slights and jealousies and ready yourself for the life beyond. Your words to others you must first apply to yourself—get your heart into harmony with Mine. What else matters?

July Twenty-ninth

Behold, to obey is better than sacrifice.

I Samuel 15:22b

Trust and obey. Trust and obey. This, My son, is the way. Your trust in Me is still too weak. You do not hear Me when I speak. Your thoughts and reasoning get in the way. They drown out most of what I say. I would commune the more with you—if all I tell you, you would do. Take heart, look up! The way is clear. Obey and trust, for I am near.

July Thirtieth

Dread came upon me, and trembling, which made all my bones shake.

Job 4:14

Mercy and grace. Mercy and grace. There is no end to My mercy and grace. Let this word remain steadfast in your heart. Cling to it when other comforts flee. Melt the hardness of rightness and let tears of gratitude flow. They water the ground from which your love will grow. My perfect love will drive away your fear. Remember, child, that I am always near.

July Thirty-first

And I am sure that He who began a good work in you will bring it to completion at the day of Jesus Christ.

Philippians 1:6

The daily portion of My word, I have given for your need. Your needs can never outrun My supply. Only your puny faith can hold back the overflowing abundance of My grace. I call you to walk this way of faith, that your spirit may grow in My likeness. The darkness of reason holds back the light of faith. Those who walk by the light of the world stumble. To walk the path I have set before you, only the light of faith will suffice. I am giving you the light of faith as a gift of My grace. Walk in it.

AUGUST

All the way my Savior leads me,
What have I to ask beside?
Can I doubt His tender mercies,
Who through life has been my guide?
Heavenly peace, divinest comfort,
Here by faith in Him to dwell,
For I know whate'er befall me,
Jesus doeth all things well.

All the way my Savior leads me,
Cheers each winding path I tread,
Gives me grace for every trial,
Feeds me with the living bread,
Though my weary steps may falter,
And my soul athirst may be,
Gushing from the Rock before me,
Lo! a spring of joy I see.

All the way my Savior leads me;
Oh, the fullness of His love!
Perfect rest to me is promised
In my Father's house above.
When my spirit, clothed immortal,
Wings its flight to realms of day,
This my song through endless ages:
Jesus led me all the way.

Fanny J. Crosby, 1820-1915

August First

For *"the earth is the Lord's, and everything in it."*

I Corinthians 10:26

From My mouth, My word goes forth to bring life to My world. This world which I created, I created in love. It is still My world. My love is eternal. My love is infinite. My life is life-giving. My word is My love. Hear My word and live. Receive My word and give. Give up the ways of death, that life may blossom forth in all its abundance. Do you not see? Life for death. That is what My love offers—not once for all, but a daily, moment-by-moment exchange: My life for your death. My way for your way. This is what My love offers My world—and you, My son.

August Second

Come, let us go up to the mountain of the Lord, to the house of the God of Jacob; that He may teach us His ways and that we may walk in His paths.

Isaiah 2:3

O foolish child! To wonder how I can speak to you and to many others at the same time! Am I not God? Did I not create this world, this universe, by the word of My power? How little you know and understand. Your demand that you understand is a block in your spiritual growth. Faith, believing, trusting—these are far more important than understanding. Understanding will come as the dawn—but it is a by-product of My light—it does not *produce* light.

Now you are hearing My voice, and yet you doubt. You wonder at these "thoughts"—which surprise you—and yet you cling to doubt. I will not remove these doubts by some spectacular miracle. I ask this of you—can you not, based on your experience of My love and poser, *choose* to abandon doubt and embrace faith? Faith is humbling. Doubt is built on pride and independence. Think about that, and choose.

August Third

He opens their ears to instruction, and commands that they return from iniquity.

Job 36:10

My child, do not despair. Your hearing is impaired. The world and all its cares have long "dinned" in your ears. Yes, you are listening for My voice. The filtering process of your mind still goes on because habits long formed do not die easily. Persevere! Do not despair. Your tears are healing, cleansing tears.

August Fourth

And the Lord said to him, "Take off the shoes from your feet, for the place where you are standing is holy ground."

Acts 7:33

This listening time is a testing time. The cares of the day continue to intrude on your mind. Will you draw aside, take off your shoes and stand on holy ground with Me? Will you make space in your busy thoughts for My thoughts? I will not intrude—under ordinary circumstances. That is My way. So if you listen—if you will *keep listening*, you will hear My voice. I, the Lord your God, am speaking in the depths of your soul. Believe and hear.

August Fifth

Before I formed you in the womb I knew you, and before you were born I consecrated you.

Jeremiah 1:5

Before you were formed, I loved you. I chose you to be a vessel and a messenger of My love. The path of your life has not been smooth. The struggles within and without I have allowed for My own purpose. Your failures have been many. Your self-love often blotted out My grace. But I did not cease to love you, for I am God—I change not. My gifts and calling are without repentance. My mercies, though

tender, are often severe—and so they have been with you. I want you
now to center on My love, and see more clearly that I do all things
well.

August Sixth

*Let not the wise man glory in his wisdom, let not the mighty man glory
in his might, let not the rich man glory in his riches; but let him who glo-
ries glory in this, that he understands and knows Me, that I am the Lord
who practices steadfast love, justice, and righteousness in the earth; for
in these things I delight, says the Lord.*

Jeremiah 9:23-24

I am not far—I have not gone away. You have separated yourself from Me by your thoughts and feelings. Your attitude toward
My servant ___ is abhorrent to Me, and results in guilt in you. You
are not called to be ___'s judge. You are called to love her and respect
her, even when you see her faults. Healing is My business— pray and
seek My love, My fatherly, paternal love, in your heart. This love will
wash away your bitter memories of the past and will enable you to
embrace fully My call on your life. Do not be afraid of this, My
child. My mercy is also toward you. You see, do you not, how much
you both need it?

August Seventh

Speak to all the cities of Judah which come to worship in the house of the Lord all the words that I command you to speak to them; do not hold back a word.

Jeremiah 26:2

You fear to write down what I am saying, because you fear being wrong. I am the Lord who healeth thee. Remember that. My word goes forth to accomplish a purpose. It is given you to hear, to bear, and to share. It is not for you alone. Like a stream of living, moving water, it gives life as it flows. My child, fear not, I am teaching you a new thing. I expect you to persist. Perfection is not yours to gain, but Mine to give. This is My word to you today.

August Eighth

In that day the deaf shall hear.

Jeremiah 29:18

I told you yesterday that you must persist. This work to which I call you is just that—work. The work of steadying your mind, quieting it before Me. It is changing the focus from thinking to listening. You are hard of hearing, but I am He who opens deaf ears. Yours is no hopeless case. Do not worry if you make mistakes, I will keep you from harm and from doing harm—that is My promise. Read over these words. They will encourage you and strengthen you to go on. Be assured I am in this process.

August Ninth

It was necessary that the word of God should be spoken first to you. Since you thrust it from you, and judge yourselves unworthy of eternal life, behold, we turn to the Gentiles.

Acts 13:46

Be of good cheer, I am the Lord who healeth thee. Do not draw back from these meeting times because you are unworthy. Worthiness is Mine to give. Your "worthiness" lies in your need. I know your tears and your fears. I bid you, My child, be of good cheer.

August Tenth

We know that in everything God works for good with those who love Him, who are called according to His purpose.

Romans 8:28

You have seen My hand at work in the circumstances of this week. I am sovereign and My will shall be done, faint hearts and frightened spirits notwithstanding. I know the thoughts of men, their motives and desires. Have I not said, "All things work together for good to those who love Me"? You will see—this is My promise—how the work is fulfilled before your very eyes.

It is easy for you now, because of what has happened, to write these words. What I look for, My child, is your willingness to write them—and believe them—when things are dark. Nevertheless, I tell you, re-read these words in the future. My sovereign will shall be done. None can stay My hand nor defeat My plan. I am the Lord.

August Eleventh

I will never fail you nor forsake you. . . . The Lord is my helper, I will not be afraid, what can man do to me?

Hebrews 13:5-6

Fear not the path I have laid out for you. Flinch not at what I ask you to bear. You will not bear it alone. Lo, I am with you, My child, in every moment. I tell you this because I know you from your conception in your mother's womb. She, too, feared many things. Your feeling of aloneness and abandonment are made more intense by your sin. The fear you feel is a punishment for your rebellion against My love. All rebellion is against My love, because I, the Lord God, am love. That is the essence of My nature. You are a creature, a creation of My love. When you understand that simple truth, you will know freedom from fear. You will know that I will never leave you nor forsake you. Never. That is My promise.

August Twelfth

The sacrifice acceptable to God is a broken spirit; a broken and contrite heart, O God, Thou wilt not despise.

Psalm 51:17

A broken and contrite heart I do not despise. There are many ways in which the heart is broken—and there is always pain when it happens. Sometimes the pain lingers and even intensifies as time goes on. Such suffering can and must be offered up to Me, My child, if its full benefit is to be realized. Let the pain of it be a continuing reminder that with the brokenness you have need for contriteness, humble repentance, meek acknowledgment, and full acceptance of your own sin. You can do this without condemnation, for I, the Lord, forgive and have forgiven. My forgiveness is absolute, but your appropriation and realization of it is dependent upon your degree of contriteness. A broken and contrite heart I do not despise.

August Thirteenth

And my God will supply every need of yours according to His riches in glory in Christ Jesus.

Philippians 4:19

There is always light enough on the path of My will for your guidance and safety. The darkness comes when you close your heart to My love and your ears to My voice. Darkness breeds the germs that weaken your body and soul. More light means more health.

My will and purpose does not change. I am the faithful One, the same today, yesterday, and for ever. Your changing moods, even your growing awareness of My will, do not change My purpose. When you fully realize and accept this, My son, you will know much greater freedom from fear than you have ever known.

There is always light enough on the path of My will for your guidance and safety.

August Fourteenth

Pour out your heart like water before the presence of the Lord!

Lamentations 2:19

Your tears are clearing the clogged channels of your mind. They are My gift to you. The past is past. I bear its burden on My heart. That, too, is My gift to you.

August Fifteenth

All things are possible to him who believes. "I believe; help my unbelief!"
Mark 8:23-24

My word is alive in you, My child, active and life-giving. I am ever faithful to keep My promises. I cannot fail you, because I am God. Not only did I hear the cry of My people in Egypt, My ears are still open to their cry. You cannot yet understand My ways. They are hidden from your sight. But I have given you enough light for your faith walk. By trusting Me where you cannot "see," your spirit grows in My likeness. Pray as the man prayed in today's gospel, "Lord, I believe; help my unbelief." I will answer that prayer.

August Sixteenth

He saved us, not because of deeds done by us in righteousness, but in virtue of His own mercy.

Titus 3:5

Springs of righteousness are flowing from My Spirit on the parched and thirsty ground of your soul. The paralyzing fear of being wrong clogs and blocks the flow of My Spirit and His life-giving power. It has nothing to do with your being "right." You have already been taught the truth of that. It has to do with inner release—inner release from the bondage of being right—the fear of being wrong.

O My child, do you not see? My righteousness covers your petty "wrongness"—and washes it away in the sea of My love. When I ask of you obedience, it is not "rightness" I seek, but the willing cooperation of your heart with My plan and path. The more you learn of Me, the more you will see the glory and the freedom I offer you. As long as you stay in your demand to be "right" to cover up your "wrongness" or to make up for it, you will continue to block the flow from the springs of righteousness that flow from and by My Spirit. Your soul will remain parched and bare. The fruit of the Spirit will be dwarfed and scanty.

O the depths of My love are yours—if you will unblock the flow! It is not yet time for all the tears to be wiped away. Their cleansing, healing work is not done. Be of good cheer, and let them flow.

August Seventeenth

The Lord is near to all who call upon Him, to all who call upon Him in truth.

Psalm 145:18

This day is a day of reckoning, of writing, of remembering. It is a day to cast aside your scruples about being wrong. They only hobble your feet and keep you from keeping time with My forward movement. It is not a day to be feared; you have spent much too much of your life in the shadow of fear. The sun is shining behind the overcast skies. You know that, and do not worry about the clouds.

It is also true in the realm of the Spirit. Uncertainty casts a cloud cover over your thoughts. But My light is still there, and you are able to walk in it—if you choose. Let the remembering today be of My mercies past. Let the reckoning be a measure of your thoughts and actions by My revealed and known will. It is not a day to be feared!

August Eighteenth

Go and say, I am ascending to My Father and your Father, to My God and your God.

John 20:17

My child, My child, I have called you My child. By this name your identity is established. I have claimed you and you are Mine—you belong to My family.

For many years, I have put My word in your mouth, but in spite of all that I did, you still did not allow your deepest identity to be realized. Instead of plunging into the deep waters, you tossed about in the shallows of ambition, fear, jealousy and rebellion. You reaped a fearsome harvest for your sin, and the results are still with you. Yet I tell you, it is time to look beyond all that—and *appropriate* My gracious gift—My love, My calling, My sovereign word: You are Mine.

August Nineteenth

There is no fear in love, but perfect love casts out fear. For fear has to do with punishment, and he who fears is not perfected in love.

I John 4:18

I am the Lord who healeth thee. I am the God of hope. My word to you today, My child, is this: Do not abandon hope! Your sight is very limited. Your interests are still very narrow. My view is larger and broader, and there is room for a lively hope in Me. My sovereign power is still able to raise the dead. My promises are still valid. My love is still from everlasting to everlasting. So cling to the realities, the truth that you have been given. Let no disturbing thoughts dislodge them from your heart. I am the God of hope, and I give you the gift of hope—if you will claim it.

August Twentieth

I give Thee thanks, O Lord, with my whole heart; before the gods I sing Thy praise.

Psalm 138:1

Set My word above all treasures of your heart. My word to you is life and breath—My Spirit's life and My divine breath. You are a bearer of My word when you are faithful to Me. It is not only for you and the life I impart to you through it. It is for others to whom

I send and intend it as well. If you keep it all to yourself, you lose half the blessing, and you rob others of the blessing I have extended to them.

"Rightly handling the word of truth"—that is your task, My son. It is not an easy task for you because of your carelessness and presumption in the past. But regrets must lead to repentance, and repentance into positive change—choices that you can and must make as you go on—to be a faithful steward of My treasure.

August Twenty-first

Wait for the Lord; be strong, and let your heart take courage; yea, wait for the Lord!

Psalm 27:14

You shall seek Me and find Me when you seek Me with all your heart. Your failure to find and hear comes from a divided and distracted heart. I will not supernaturally take away this condition. It is one that you must learn to hate, and to hate the bitter fruit it bears. When you have tired of it, and the spiritual torpor that results, you will be willing to pay the price: *Then* you will find My presence and My reality. I don't curse your lethargy, but neither do I condone it. Thank you.

August Twenty-second

You will seek Me and find Me, when you seek Me with all your heart.
Jeremiah 29:13

And now, My son, hear this word: Your prayer is heard and you can cast all your cares on Me. I will not fail you and will keep My word. My healing is still going on, and I have not forgotten you. Remember the joy of the Lord is your strength. So even now beforehand rejoice in Me. It *is* a good thing to rejoice and give thanks. You can never out-test My love and goodness.

August Twenty-third

Jesus the pioneer and perfecter of our faith, who for the joy that was set before Him endured the cross, despising the shame, and is seated at the right hand of the throne of God.
Hebrews 12:2

Is My arm shortened that it cannot save? Is My ear deaf to the cry of My children? You do not need to hide in shame over sins and mistakes of the past. I bore your shame on the cross that you might be spared. Yet you have lived long in shame and have not allowed My grace and mercy to cover you.

This present onslaught is an opportunity for you to "despise the shame." This has been a weak point in you, and would have been even more harmful if I had not intervened. Claim the covert of My wings, and know that I am God. Claim the cleansing blood and seek deeper repentance. But "despise the shame" of this attack. Have I not commanded thee?

August Twenty-fourth

First take the log out of your own eye, and then you will see clearly to take the speck out of your brother's eye.

Matthew 7:5

You are not better than those who have fallen into great temptation. I have kept you in the hollow of My hand when your own nature would have led you to paths of destruction for you and those you love. Be always aware of this. My love and My sovereign power have kept and guarded your way.

August Twenty-fifth

I sought the Lord, and He answered me, and delivered me from all my fears.
Psalm 34:4

Go forward in the strength that I give you. Your strength must fail that Mine may prevail. The weakening you feel is not a negative thing. It is a door into a more intimate walk with Me. Your independence has cost you much. This new dependence growing from your weakness will serve you well if you will come to peace with it. Continue to pray—and let your prayers be stronger, larger, bolder—and I will be glorified through them.

August Twenty-sixth

And whatever you ask in prayer, you will receive, if you have faith.
Matthew 21:22

My dear child, you worry and fret about many foolish things, and thereby lose your peace. This is not necessary, for there is an abundance of peace available to you now, if you are open to it. When you allow your old nature to rise up in jealousy of your brethren, in fear of losing "place" or being replaced—peace is sacrificed on the altar of pride. This is not a light thing but a serious condition that I choose to address. Together, My child, let us journey into a *new* place—a place of satisfaction *and* peace.

August Twenty-seventh

There are those who rebel against the light, who are not acquainted with its ways, and do not stay in its paths.

Job 25:13

Be still, be still and know that I am speaking! Your knowledge of Me is still shallow and immature. Yet your days are full of years and you have had more than ample opportunities to "grow in grace and in the knowledge of Me." I have dealt with you in much mercy and loving kindness. Your weakness is My gift to you, and My weapon against your innate arrogance.

I will not withdraw My loving kindness to you. That is My sovereign, unchangeable promise. Listen and be ready to fulfill My design. It is good.

August Twenty-eighth

I will turn their mourning into joy, I will comfort them, and give them gladness for sorrow.

Jeremiah 31:13

Hearken to My voice, O blessed child of Mine. Hear the words of comfort that I speak within. Yes, I am the builder of ruins—the ruins that resulted from your wrong choices and wandering ways. These ruins are not only in your own life—they are also consequences you neither foresaw nor feared. I sanctify My name in those I claim, and I will be glorified in My work. I am the builder of ruins.

August Twenty-ninth

Draw near to God and He will draw near to you.

James 4:8

I am calling you to a new level of responsibility, guard it well. I am giving you the opportunity to speak with wisdom and understanding. Guard it well. Keep your sin confessed and beware the pitfalls of substituting your will and way for Mine. But be courageous, My son, and do not fail in this task. Be assured that I will not fail you nor these people whom I love.

August Thirtieth

God chose to make known how great among the Gentiles are the riches of the glory of this mystery, which is Christ in you, the hope of glory.

Colossians 1:27

My child, do not despair when past sins rise up to accuse you. Their memory is a reminder of the seriousness of disobedience against Me. You often ignored the inner restraints I set upon you, and forgot the long-term consequences on your soul. Continue to repent in the depth of your heart, for the broken and contrite heart is one that can receive My healing. The hard, impenitent heart beats on to its own destruction.

All is well. In Me is plenteous redemption. I have not failed you and will *not*.

August Thirty-first

Jesus Christ is the same yesterday and today and for ever.

Hebrews 13:8

Look to Me in good times as well as bad. Your understanding of My ways needs both. I never afflict My children aimlessly—and with each trial, I prepare a blessing. Your emotions are fickle, changeable as waves on the sea. My love for you is constant, and no matter what the "weather" is, it remains steady and sure.

SEPTEMBER

Jesus shall reign where'er the sun
    Does his successive journeys run;
His kingdom stretch from shore to shore
    Till moons shall wax and wane no more.

For Him shall endless prayer be made,
    And praises throng to crown His head;
His name, like sweet perfume, shall rise
    With every morning sacrifice.

People and realms, of every tongue,
    Dwell on His love with sweetest song;
And infant voices shall proclaim
    Their early blessings on His name.

Blessings abound where'er He reigns;
    The prisoner leaps to lose his chains;
The weary find eternal rest,
    And all the sons of want are blest.

Let every creature rise and bring
    Peculiar honors to our King;
Angels descend with songs again,
    And earth repeat the loud Amen.

Isaac Watts, 1719

September First

Praise the Lord! Praise the Lord, O my soul! I will praise the Lord as long as I live; I will sing praises to my God while I have being.

Psalm 146:1

Praise is the key that unlocks the treasure store of My mercies. Numberless blessings are available to those who learn the secret of praise. As a flower unfolds before the sun, to receive its life-giving rays, so the soul opens before Me through the act of praise. There is no life without light—and the soul that does not praise continues in its lifeless darkness.

Dwell in My life-giving light, My child, with a continuing attitude of praise and thanksgiving. Praise is the key that unlocks the treasure store of My mercies.

September Second

For I know the plans I have for you, says the Lord, plans for welfare and not for evil, to give you a future and a hope.

Jeremiah 29:11

My dear child, the valleys, as well as the hills, are Mine also. Do not wonder that your path takes the lowlands as well as the high. I am with you in the desert as well as in the garden. To know this is life indeed.

Be not afraid of tomorrow. All your tomorrows are known and planned by Me—the Architect of Time. I know the plans I have for you—plans of good and not of evil. Let your heart be open to My goodness.

September Third

For the sake of your tradition, you have made void the word of God. . . . In vain do you worship Me, teaching as doctrines the precepts of men.
From Matthew 15:6, 9

I, the Lord your God, am speaking to you. My Spirit within carries My word to My children. This is a living relationship. It is not made up of theories and propositions, but of *life*—My life within your life.

In the past, you did not understand this, and in spite of the hunger of your heart, you clung to ideas and doctrines. It is not that the doctrines were false, but they could not provide what you needed and longed for without knowing it. I have shown you in remembering glimpses of this hunger you felt.

Do not wonder at the reasons why I allowed the years to pass in this way. Remember, My child, that I work with My children in wisdom and mercy—and I know when to intervene and when to withhold. My view of life is very different from yours. Only as you come to see with My vision will you understand. In the meantime, trust Me to give or withhold—in My greater wisdom and love.

September Fourth

Then all men will fear; they will tell what God has wrought and ponder what He has done. Let the righteous rejoice in the Lord, and take refuge in Him! Let all the upright in heart glory.

Psalm 64:9-10

My dear child, you are dear to Me. Listen with your heart and I will help you deal with your fears. You do not need to know what lies ahead. I know, and that is enough. Your path will always have light if you stay close to Me in your heart. Listen more faithfully. Light rises in the darkness for the upright.

September Fifth

Thus says the Lord: "Stand by the roads, and look, and ask for the ancient paths, where the good way is; and walk in it, and find rest for your souls."

Jeremiah 6:16

Eternal peace abides in My presence. Know that here is rest from turmoil and a cure for the restlessness of your heart. Seek this peace more frequently, My son, for in it lies My healing, My wisdom, and My strength.

September Sixth

All flesh is grass, and all its beauty is like the flower of the field. The grass withers, the flower fades, when the breath of the Lord blows upon it; surely the people is grass. The grass withers, the flower fades; but the word of our God will stand for ever.

Isaiah 40:6b-8

In My sovereign love I have chosen you. Not because you are or were "lovable" but because I chose to love you. Your life is a demonstration of My mercy. You have yet to understand the full meaning of this, but you do catch glimpses of it. You still want to take credit for the good I work in you. But this cannot be because it denies the basic truth of your life. In My sovereign love I chose to love you.

September Seventh

To set the mind on the flesh is death, but to set the mind on the Spirit is life and peace.

Romans 8:6

In the quietness I speak. In the noise of your thoughts and words you cannot hear. Learn to be quiet. I have called you and commissioned you to a task too great for you. Only as you *listen* will you be able to fulfill your task. I will not forsake you nor let you bring harm to My work. But to fulfill your call, you *must* hear and heed what I say. Your fear of being wrong stops your ears from hearing. And eph-phatha! Be opened!

September Eighth

I know that nothing good dwells within me, that is, in my flesh. I can will what is right, but I cannot do it.

Romans 7:18

You will continue to be led by thoughts that I put into your mind. You cannot always be sure such thoughts are from Me, and you know the danger of confusing your opinions with My will. When your suggestions are refused, you find it humiliating and painful, because you are not free simply to release them into My keeping. Be more bold without demanding that every new thought "hit the target" and find approval. I will sort out the dross from the gold, and your obedience will work blessing both for you and for others.

September Ninth

Make me to know Thy ways, O Lord; teach me Thy paths. Lead me in Thy truth, and teach me.

Psalm 25:4-5a

The manna of the day is My word to you. Sufficient unto the day—but you are always in need of fresh supply. Do not fear or reject these words which come to you and to others, for they bring life to the spirit. They do not supplant My holy word which you love, but you do not need to be jealous for it. You are doing right to insist on its primacy, but you are wrong in resisting the fresh word which quickens the spirit of My children. I will guard My truth. The Spirit of truth has been given you and He will protect His own. So receive My gift—the gift of My love to you—and do not fear!

September Tenth

Esau . . . sold his birthright to Jacob. . . . Thus Esau despised his birthright.

Genesis 25:32-34

You have lost much ground through your neglect in listening to Me. Quelling the busy mind with its rebellious thoughts takes effort and practice. You are still at the beginning stage in this effort, and have little understanding of what success will require. But do not let that discourage you, for I am faithful, even when your faithlessness puts a barrier between us. My dear child, do not sell your birthright for a mess of pottage. Claim the prize I hold before you. It is more precious than gold.

September Eleventh

So Peter got out of the boat and walked on the water and came to Jesus; but when he saw the wind, he was afraid, and beginning to sink he cried out, "Lord, save me." Jesus immediately reached out his hand and caught him, saying to him, "O man of little faith, why did you doubt?"
Matthew 14:29b-31

My child, I am with you always. You are never alone, even when you feel alone. The depths are Mine as well as the heights. No waters can drown those who are in My care. Too many times you look at the "waters"—the circumstances which contain pain and seem to threaten your very life. But these are trials of your trust in Me. If you do not trust Me then, when can you? Do not waste the dry times, the "lonely" times when I seem far away. Let them acquaint you with the deeper truth that "underneath are the everlasting arms."

September Twelfth

Into Thy hand I commit my spirit; Thou hast redeemed me, O Lord, faithful God.

Psalm 31:5

Go about the day calmly and without hurry. In the midst of much bustle, keep a quiet spirit. Let your word of encouragement be a source of peace to others. Be generous in your encouragement and expressions of appreciation. Cement relations with the bond of love. I will be with you and remind you of this.

September Thirteenth

Say to those who are of a fearful heart, "Be strong, fear not! Behold, your God will come with vengeance, with the recompense of God. He will come and save you."

Isaiah 35:4

I am the Lord who has redeemed you. I am acquainted with all your ways. Your tears and fears are not hidden from Me. Your hopes and prayers are not forgotten.

Time is also My servant. I make a way in the desert where there is no way. My glory is revealed in the small details of your daily life, not just the big deliverances and miracles. Blessed are those with eyes to see and hearts to understand the workings of My fatherly love and care.

September Fourteenth

A new commandment I give to you, that you love one another; even as I have loved you, that you also love one another.

John 13:34

I have heard your cry and your words of love. Have you heard Mine—in the depths of your soul? Mine is a constant love—neither waxing nor waning with the changing circumstances. Yours blows hot or cold, and is still far from pure. Your many distractions demonstrate the unstableness of your affections. Yet I do not despise your love—and do not want you to be discouraged by its fickleness. Press on, My child, and see greater wonders of My love, for My thoughts are for good and not for ill. Have I not told you?

September Fifteenth

I do not occupy myself with things too great and too marvelous for me. But I have calmed and quieted my soul.

Psalm 131:1b-2a

Yes, child, you may lean on Me. My heart is open to you, My ear is attuned to your cry. Marvel not that this is so, and do not wonder about "things too high for you." My mercies never run short, they endure forever. Those who know My name, those whom I have called by name, are vessels of mercy. Taste here the sweetness of My fatherly love. Give over your understanding and receive it as a little child. The wilderness way is hard. Welcome here, My child. You may lean on Me.

September Sixteenth

Come, let us go up to the mountain of the Lord, to the house of the God of Jacob; that He may teach us His ways and that we may walk in His paths.

Isaiah 2:3b

I have called you to walk close to Me. Only here is your safety. You cannot be trusted to wander far afield, for your nature is too strongly attached to its old ways. Here, at My side, you can taste the sweetness of My kingdom, and wean yourself from the intoxicating pull of the world.

You have much to learn about obedience, about listening to the still, small voice of My Spirit, which will direct your path--if you will learn to listen and obey. For your own sake, My child, practice and learn.

September Seventeenth

What does the Lord require of you but to do justice, and to love kindness, and to walk humbly with your God?

Micah 6:8b

Blessed are those whom I call to walk with Me. Blessed are those who hear My voice and heed it. Their paths are the path of life, for I am the life of the faithful ones. You have heard My call, and have stumbled along the way. Yours has been an unsteady walk, for you preferred your own thoughts and dreams. Your suffering is a necessary purgation of spirit, that you may learn to walk upright and steady along My path.

Blessed are those whom I call to walk with Me.

September Eighteenth

Let the words of my mouth and the meditation of my heart be acceptable in Thy sight, O Lord, my rock and my redeemer.

Psalm 19:14

I am with you always, even to the end. My gentle voice is easily drowned out with the cluttering of your own thoughts and earthly concerns. Listen more intently—do not grow discouraged or give up. This is all a part of maturing in Me—and a preparation for the future.

I am putting My words in your mouth and in your mind. By faith, you can receive them, speak and hear them. Do not worry about getting them "right." That is pride. I will not allow you to stray too far. Trust Me.

September Nineteenth

Love does no wrong to a neighbor; therefore love is the fulfilling of the law.

Romans 13:10

There is no fear in love. As your love for Me grows, you will find that fear lessens. My wrath is against sin—not against persons. When you persist in sin, My wrath will be felt. But it is meant to turn you away from sin and its consequent fear—to My welcoming love. This is not sentimentality. It is an eternal truth.

Concentrate, therefore, on My unfathomable love. Your heart has long responded to this dimension of the gospel, but your growth was stunted in many ways. It is time to move on, trusting Me each step of the way—to open doors, to shed light on the path, to lead, to turn and to reward your faltering steps of obedience. Let the latter part of your journey be better than the former. The old has passed away. Let it be. Come with Me, My child, and learn love's way. It is a good way, and blessed are those who walk in it.

September Twentieth

You did not choose Me, but I chose you and appointed you that you should go and bear fruit.

John 15:16a

My son, I will be found when you seek Me with your whole heart from a clearly felt need of Me. I will not be used for hidden agendas—so beware of them when you come to these moments of listening. No familiarity will ever destroy the distance between Creator and creature. You know your lifelong tendency to presumptuousness. Approach My throne with due humility and a willingness to be shown the wounds and scars that still deface your soul. I rebuke those whom I love and chasten every son.

September Twenty-first

Gracious is the Lord, and righteous; our God is merciful. The Lord preserves the simple; when I was brought low, He saved me.

Psalm 116:5-6

My dear child, you worry about things too high for you. You delve into mysteries that must remain mysteries—and you are not satisfied to leave them at that. Rest your mind in the simplicity of the faith I have planted in you, and do not fret about these larger questions. Leave them to Me to sort out. You have all the light you need to walk with Me day by day. That is enough.

September Twenty-second

I will restore to you the years which the locust has eaten.

Joel 2:25

These little personal talks which I vouchsafe to give you are manifestations of My Fatherly love and care for you. They are still breaking up the inward hard places, making your spirit more pliable and leadable. That is no small gift, My son, and I bid you treasure it. I have led you to writing them down so that you may refer to them again and again. But the reading of past conversations is not meant to replace the ongoing live ones. At the present time this is about as much as you can stand.

September Twenty-third

Be still before the Lord, and wait patiently for Him. . . . Fret not yourself; it tends only to evil.

Psalm 37:7-8

Wait on the Lord and do not fret when no words come. Patience is necessary if you are to complete your course with joy. Let no silence cause you to think that I am absent. Rather let the silence increase your thirst for the living water. Keep on seeking, keep on asking—for in the process, I am doing a necessary work in you. Remember, you are still in spiritual "kindergarten."

September Twenty-fourth

Behold, I am with you and will keep you wherever you go, and will bring you back to this land; for I will not leave you until I have done that of which I have spoken to you.

Genesis 28:15

My own are those who hear My word and do it. My own are those whose hearts have responded to My heart of love. They are a chosen band, a royal priesthood, and I look to them to intercede on behalf of those whose hearts are still cold and lifeless.

September Twenty-fifth

Cast all your anxieties on Him, for He cares about you.

I Peter 5:7

In the secret place I meet with My own. Not the words that come to you, but My presence. Not your thoughts but My merciful loving kindness. The words are outward shells to hold the inner reality in visible form. They can remind you in the future of our meeting here, My child. You have found a great and priceless secret in your latter years: the sure mercies of David—the sweetness of My sovereign love.

September Twenty-sixth

The scripture says, "No one who believes in Him will be put to shame."
Romans 10:11

My son, when I speak, your fear of "getting it wrong" interferes with our communication. You must not wait for some overwhelming assurance that you are really hearing, but follow more readily the "small voice" within. I, too, want there to be the sweet goings in and out between us, the comfortable relationship that allows that sense of rest. You still hold Me "at arm's length"—afraid of looking foolish to others—afraid of being confounded. Have I not given you enough evidence that you can move on?

September Twenty-seventh

I glorified Thee on earth, having accomplished the work which Thou gavest Me to do.
John 17:4

Let your heart be glad and rejoice in Me, My son, for your prayer is heard and your sin is forgiven. Your pride is still your greatest fault, and you must cooperate with Me if it is to be given the death-blow needed. You do not need to fear, though I know this is what you feel at such a suggestion. You have already received the most painful stroke—and it had to be for your sake. Learn to hate the pride and see its "pleasure" as an addiction to be overcome. My love and presence are infinitely to be preferred.

September Twenty-eighth

I was sent to speak to you, and to bring you this good news.
Luke 1:19b

Keep listening for My voice throughout your day. I speak not only in the listening time, but often in your daily work. *You* must become more accustomed to My voice, My child. Ours is not meant to be a "by appointment only" relationship, but one of walking together, day and night. Keep listening and that relationship will develop.

September Twenty-ninth

For Thou, O Lord, art my hope, my trust, O Lord, from my youth.
Psalm 71:5

Bitterness blocks the working of My Spirit. When you entertain bitter feelings you drive out the Spirit of grace. Left in that darkness, you feel dead, lifeless, and heavy. No matter what the provocation, your recourse to bitterness is inexcusable—and for you, foolish. You know better, but you indulge this part of your nature and sink into the mire of self-pity and vindictiveness. Give up the demand that others treat you in "a certain way" and learn from Me.

September Thirtieth

My grace is sufficient for you, for My power is made perfect in weakness.
II Corinthians 12:9a

Think not that all is lost. What man cannot do, I am able to achieve. Your sense of hopelessness and despair lead nowhere. Faith in My sovereign power and goodness leads to change and growth. My purpose in your life is still in process. You are merely partway to life's goal. All the inconsistencies and incompleteness are being resolved in My way and according to My schedule. This is true for you and your house. "There shall no evil befall you, neither shall any plague come nigh thy dwelling." Take that word for you and yours.

OCTOBER

The ancient law departs
        And all its terrors cease;
For Jesus makes with faithful hearts
        A covenant of peace.

The Light of Light divine,
        True brightness undefiled,
He bears for us the shame of sin,
        A holy, spotless Child.

Today the Name is thine,
        At which we bend the knee;
They call Thee Jesus, Child divine!
        Our Jesus deign to be.

Sebastian Besnault, 1736

October First

How sweet are Thy words to my taste, sweeter than honey to my mouth!
Psalm 119:103

Guard the words that I give you with loving care. They are given first and primarily for your own good. You must not use them as an ego builder, as a way of making yourself special. Like food for the hungry, the words that I speak are food and nourishment for your soul. Like medicine, they bring healing to the soul's wounds.

Long have I waited for you, My child, to seek and find, to accept My offer to hold communion with you. Guarding the time and keeping yourself in readiness to hear are an important way to "Guard the words that I give you with loving care."

October Second

Teach me good judgment and knowledge, for I believe in Thy commandments.

Psalm 119:66

Hearken to Me, My dear son, and listen attentively. Learn to look with the eyes of the spirit beyond the outer shell. Let your thoughts and your words aim at what lies hidden from the natural view, and do not be confused by it. I will give you the discernment you need in order to minister life. Remember that My love and care go beyond any immediate problems. Pray that you may see with Me the long view—the good to which I am leading each child of Mine. Too much attention on the single incident can cloud that vision and cause unnecessary problems.

October Third

It is your Father's good pleasure to give you the kingdom.

Luke 12:32*b*

No one waits for Me in vain I am He who keeps promises. Do not let yourself grow weary when I seem to delay. There is good reason for it, even if you never know what it is. Trust is not built on knowledge of details. Trust is in the character of the One in whom you choose to believe. I have given you more than ample evidence of who I am, My son. I am not playing games with you as a pawn. He who waits for Me will not be confounded. That is My sovereign promise. Be at peace.

October Fourth

God is at work in you, both to will and to work for His good pleasure.
Philippians 2:13

Your children are in My care. I will never let them go. You have seen already how I can change circumstances and move in the hidden depths of hearts. Never doubt My faithfulness. Never let circumstances shake your faith that I will keep My solemn word. Keep praying and keep believing. There will yet be a happy issue from all your afflictions.

October Fifth

The light shines in the darkness, and the darkness has not overcome it.
John 1:5

I am speaking in the silence. Wordless words come from My Spirit to yours—wordless to your mind but not to your spirit. There in the secret place I build My dwelling. Guard it well, My child. Suffer no strange fires upon the altar of your heart. Heed the warning signs, the nudging of My Spirit when tempted to serve another god.

October Sixth

The Lord is gracious and merciful, slow to anger and abounding in steadfast love. The Lord is good to all, and His compassion is over all that He has made.

Psalm 145:8-9

I have told you that the year ahead will bring many surprises. Not all of them will be pleasant, but *all* of them will be in the compass of My mercy. They will bring blessing and I want you to be prepared to look for and recognize the blessing.

Discount the nay-saying spirits. No worthwhile achievement is ever accomplished without struggle and questions. Present vision is but partial and very incomplete. Keep open to have your eyes refocused and the vision made more clear. I am still revealing My plan, even in the delays and the necessary changes. But do not lose heart. I will not fail you.

October Seventh

The Lord is just in all His ways, and kind in all His doings.

Psalm 145:17

The hollow of My hand is not always easy to recognize. My leadings may seem strange and even unloving to you. But I have kept you safe from the enemy's designs and have tolerated your rebellion against My will. Your murmurings and inward complaints are not hidden from Me. I know where you are safest and most blessed—you do not, and it is My grace that holds you back.

October Eighth

Every good . . . and every perfect gift is from above, coming down from the Father of lights with Whom there is no variation or shadow due to change.

James 1:17

I have promised and I will fulfill. I have spoken and I will do that which I have said. There is neither variableness nor shadow of turning with Me. All things are present to My view, and My wisdom encompasses every circumstance and event. The shadows in your life are cast by your own self, standing between My light and the concern you have. By stepping aside, and allowing My light to shine on the situation, you will be able to see and understand much that now remains dark and uncertain.

October Ninth

Be still before the Lord, and wait patiently for Him.

Psalm 37:7a

Waiting is good, My son. It is healing and purifying, for it reveals your unsteady and unfocused life. Waiting is necessary, for in your impatience you would grab a few words and dash off to your own agenda. I am offering you words of life. They are not cheap, nor are they to be treated so. Waiting is part of the price I ask of you, to show the earnestness of your desire for them and your willingness to value them highly.

Blessed is he whose mind is stayed on Me. You have a long way to go before your mind learns to *stay* itself on Me. But do not lose heart. Wait for the Lord. Be of good courage, and *I* will strengthen your heart.

October Tenth

Let Thy work be manifest to Thy servants, and Thy glorious power to their children.

Psalm 90:16

There are new plans to be unfolded, new provisions to be made. New mercies to be revealed. Live expectantly. Put aside murmurings and discontent—that My goodness may be experienced. Your negative attitude is a hindrance and offense. It contradicts what you say you believe about Me. From the same fountain you give sweet and bitter water.

I want you to give special attention to this sin-tendency and conquer it. Ask others to help you and forego the dark pleasure you get from it.

October Eleventh

[Paul and Barnabas returned,] strengthening the souls of the disciples, exhorting them to continue in the faith, and saying that through many tribulations we must enter the kingdom of God.

Acts 14:22

The rainbow is a sign of promise—an inward sign that My promises shall be fulfilled. The delays and detours are but opportunities for you to "keep on believing." That is what Abraham did, beyond any reason to believe, except for My promise. Such faith is still a rare thing, and I rejoice when any child of Mine chooses it.

October Twelfth

Let us then with confidence draw near to the throne of grace, that we may receive mercy and find grace to help in time of need.

Hebrews 4:16

I am here, My dear child, even though you do not see nor "feel" My presence. Your fears and your tears are not hidden from My eyes. These "low" times where there is no feeling of victory and little of joy are all part of My perfect plan. I do not cause them in you, but it is My will to use them for your good. They penetrate beneath the shallow and surface "joy" you would choose, and drive your roots deeper into the mystery of My suffering love. Stay close to Me, My son. I am very near to you.

October Thirteenth

Do not neglect the gift you have, which was given you by prophetic utterance when the elders laid their hands upon you.

I Timothy 4:14

This is a day of reckoning. This is a day of mercy. No evil shall befall you, neither shall any plague come nigh thy dwelling. My ways are not your ways and My thoughts are not your thoughts. You are centered in a small world of self-concern. My world encompasses a multitude of generations—and yet I include you in it. Do not fear My judgments, for they are for your good. Let My will become yours and you will have greater peace.

October Fourteenth

Do not quench the Spirit.

I Thessalonians 5:19a

I have told you that the waiting is part of My plan. Work is going on in your soul even while you wait a quickening word from Me. There are many wasted years behind you, and it is My will to restore what has been lost. For this I require your patience and your cooperation. You cannot change the past. The fruit and consequences of your decisions are part of the reality of your life. But as we work together in the restoration, we work against the intent of the adversary to bring you and others into condemnation. The process requires patience—and trust.

October Fifteenth

Our hope for you is unshaken; for we know that as you share in our sufferings, you will also share in our comfort.

II Corinthians 1:7

My dear son, you are still filled with fear. I cannot use you as I would while this is the case, because your fear puts a separation between us. The separation is on your side, not Mine. I have told you that you will face nothing without My divine aid. Yet you allow the smallest indication of possible trouble to bring consternation to your heart. I do not ask you to be brave. I ask you to *trust me*! I rebuke your craven fear and tell you it is not necessary or inevitable. You give the enemy a cheap victory when you entertain these faithless fears.

October Sixteenth

Therefore, since we are surrounded by so great a cloud of witnesses, let us lay aside every weight, and sin which clings so closely, and let us run with perseverance the race that is set before us.

Hebrews 12:1

Echoes of eternity. My sheep hear My voice and I know them, and they follow Me. Few listen, but I am faithful, and those who wait for Me shall not be confounded. Seek clarity amid confusion. Seek quietness of soul. Seek conviction of your sins and be made whole.

October Seventeenth

So neither he who plants nor he who waters is anything, but only God who gives the growth.

I Corinthians 3:7

I plant and move and pluck up. I water and bring forth fruit in its season. But tending the plant I leave in part to you. The necessary prunings I bring about in various ways but I ask for your willing assent. "Let it be unto me according to your word," as did Mary of Nazareth. It was as hard for her to say yes to My plan as it has ever been for you. You can see how I used her assent to further My redemptive design. You cannot see how I will make use of yours. The prunings are first for your own sake, and then to make useful in My kingdom the fruit your life will bear.

October Eighteenth

Each man's work will become manifest; for the Day will disclose it, because it will be revealed with fire, and the fire will test what sort of work each one has done.

I Corinthians 3;13

Insights are given by My Spirit to enable you to walk more faithfully in the path I have laid out for you. Past faithlessness has cost you many a victory, and you have suffered loss—throwing in hay, wood and stubble, when I offered you gold, silver and precious stones. You have excused yourself from hard places when you *could* have *stood* and served Me. Do try to learn from the past so that in the time of testing, you will make better choices. "No arm so weak but may do service here." This includes yours. All you risk is a little pain—an unpleasant incident, the threat of losing someone's favor and good opinion. Let your new insight *work* for you, My child.

October Nineteenth

Bless the Lord, O my soul, and forget not all His benefits, who forgives all your iniquity, and heals all your diseases.

Psalm 103:2-3

In giving you the light for one step at a time I spare you many burdens. Since the future is Mine, it is no burden to Me, for I know the plans I have for you. But you would be frightened and burdened if you could see too far ahead. Tracing the memories and mercies of the past can gird your soul with strength for "the next step." Fear not what it shall be, My child. I have not forgotten to be gracious.

October Twentieth

Let my tongue cleave to the roof of my mouth, if I do not remember you, if I do not set Jerusalem above my highest joy!

Psalm 137:6

My child, do not forget to bear on your heart the little ones I have given in your care. Your faithful prayer is a kind of care, and a lax and careless spirit can be costly. The enemy is hard at work to keep light from dispelling the delusions he offers. Faithful, persistent prayer penetrates that and allows truth to be seen. I have called you to this burden and task. Do not fail.

October Twenty-first

Restore to me the joy of Thy salvation, and uphold me with a willing spirit.
Psalm 51:12

The enemy is at work in your attempted plans. Your own lack of awareness of his strategy and capacity for mischief is reflected in your lack of covering prayer. Be more humble and dependent on prayer to solve the problem and more ready to pray over "small," ordinary things than you have been. Prayer is still an unexplored country for you. Let this be a "wake-up call"!

October Twenty-second

For you are all sons of light and sons of the day; we are not of the night or of darkness.

1 Thessalonians 5:5

The words I speak to you are more than "words." They are spirit and life. They come with the very fine power of My life and do not depend on your getting every "word" right. They come to edify, to build up your spirit. You know that without Me you are weak and cannot stand. I know that, too, but I do not despise your weakness. It is far better than the false strength you tried so hard to cultivate. Be content, My child, to remain dependent on My daily supply. Remember the widow's cruse of oil that did not fail.

October Twenty-third

I know whom I have believed and I am sure that he is able to guard until that Day what has been entrusted to me.

II Timothy 1:12b

Dull and listless. Dull and listless, wrapped up in your own little world, when the greatness and glory of My world are waiting for you to experience! A little pain and discomfort throws you into a complete shutting down of faith and shutting into your fearful, dull self-absorption. Your cage is of your own making, as you seek to protect yourself against the fears you have fed and nourished. Away with this folly, My son! Rally the things that remain and sally forth to *life* this day in the fullness of My life—not in the dullness of yours.

October Twenty-fourth

For it is not you who speak, but the Spirit of your Father speaking through you.

Matthew 10:20

O fearful one, fear not to go forward in sharing the words entrusted to you. They are not your words but Mine, and they will not return to Me void. Do not worry about calling them My words, because I am doing a work in you and through you in this process. Mine will be the glory, not yours, and that is your safety—I will keep you hidden in My hand of love. It is the only safe place for you.

October Twenty-fifth

Surely goodness and mercy shall follow me all the days of my life; and I shall dwell in the house of the Lord for ever.

Psalm 23:6

Fear not to take hold of the plow—the work I have set before you. Pray for My wisdom in dealing with the questions that come before you. Although they may *seem* impossible to your eye, remember that I deal in "impossibilities" and that there is an answer.

Prayer is a weapon against the present attack of the adversary. Encourage My people to take it more seriously. It is not a pious exercise. It is a battle waged against spiritual darkness and wickedness.

October Twenty-sixth

Again Jesus spoke to them, saying, "I am the light of the world; he who follows Me will not walk in darkness, but will have the light of life."

John 8:12

I have called you from your mother's womb to be Mine. I have strewn the path of your life with mercies and blessings. My hand has restrained you and kept you from the path of destruction. Even now I am rehearsing lessons begun many years ago which you have not yet mastered. Those whom I call I chasten. My mercies may seem severe, but I ask you to look back and see, look back and give thanks. And be sure, My son, that I never ask you to bear more than you are able—by My divine help and presence.

October Twenty-seventh

No eye has seen, nor ear heard, nor the heart of man conceived, what God has prepared for those who love Him.

I Corinthians 2:9

Sometimes I speak in the silence, My son. Wordless silence. I communicate with your spirit instead of your mind. This is not less, but more a life-giving word to you. Be content to allow Me to choose how I shall convey what you need.

In the course of time you will see unfolding wonders greater than you can imagine. In the course of time you will see the harvest of your prayers. In the course of time, you will behold My glory revealed in the fulfillment of My promises. I am the true and faithful One. Keep on praying. Keep on weeping. Keep on trusting. Keep on hoping. You will not be confounded.

October Twenty-eighth

Every one who asks receives, and he who seeks finds, and to him who knocks it will be opened.

Matthew 7:8

My son, listen to My word, forming words in your mind. I have chosen this form of communication to accommodate your need. In order to receive it you must suspend your doubts and questioning, and *trust* beyond your understanding.

I am still in the process of breaking up stony areas on your soul—hardenings you have long since forgotten. When I renew a soul, it requires a time of mourning as well as a rebirth of joy and hope. Acquaint yourself with all of them—and with Me.

October Twenty-ninth

May those who sow in tears reap with shouts of joy!

Psalm 126:5

My son, I have not called you to walk a lonely path of briars and thorns. I have called you out of the briars and thorns of your natural way into a path of inward peace. As yet you have only faintly realized My purposes, for you carry your briars and thorns with you— your pride and lust for recognition and praise. Seek peace and pursue it actively and aggressively. I do not mean a passive, lazy peace, but one that reflects and expresses My peace—acceptance of My will when you cannot understand, believing that everything that comes into your life is by My loving will or loving consent. Take the dread and foreboding about the future and offer it up to Me. I am *with* you. I cannot fail you. Peace, true peace, rests on the bedrock of My love.

October Thirtieth

None of those who take refuge in Him will be condemned.

Psalm 34:22b

It is not necessary, My child, to have feelings of any particular kind in these listening times. The important thing is steadiness, faithfulness, perseverance. My will and desire are unchanging, make no mistake about that. I have declared it to all My children, and would that they would believe and act on it. But to those who "have an ear to hear," I am more than ready to speak. Your difficulty lies in part in feeling that it will be necessary to have certain *feelings* before you can trust what you hear. Trust more and do not be so afraid of being wrong!

October Thirty-first

The fear of the Lord is instruction in wisdom, and humility goes before honor.

Proverbs 15:33

Light arises in the darkness for those who love Me. No threat can thwart the ongoing fulfillment of My will. Say to those of a fearful heart: Behold your king! Have I failed you in the past? Has My help been withheld from your cry? Let everything conspire to propel you forward in the path I have laid out for you. No, you cannot see the "distant end," but there is light on your path today. Keep your eye on the light and the darkness will lose its power to trouble you.

NOVEMBER

Give praise and glory unto God,
　　The Father of all blessing;
His mighty wonders tell abroad,
　　His graciousness confessing.
With balm my inmost heart He fills,
　　His comfort all my anguish stills.
To God be praise and glory.

The host of heaven praiseth Thee,
　　O Lord of all dominions;
And mortal men, on land and sea,
　　Beneath Thy shadowing pinions,
Exult in Thy creative might
　　That doeth all things well and right.
To God be praise and glory.

What God hath wrought to show His power
　　He evermore sustaineth;
He watches o'er us every hour,
　　His mercy never waneth.
Through all His kingdom's wide domain,
　　His righteousness and glory reign.
To God be praise and glory.

J.J. Schuetz, 1675

November First

But truly God has listened; He has given heed to the voice of my prayer.
Psalm 66:19

Your prayers, though feeble and imperfect, are a source of joy to My heart. This is because your prayers release the power I have bound in them—allowing prayer to become a vital part of My mercy supply. I could effect everything without prayer, but that would deprive My children of the dignity I have bestowed in this gift. Prayer is not a beggar asking bread from an unwilling God. Prayer is the exercise of Throne-rights by God's children. Of course they are a source of joy to Me, because I rejoice when My children *act* like My children—and in the process *become* more completely what I have meant them to be. Pray seriously, My child—but pray *joyfully*.

November Second

Let the righteous rejoice in the Lord, and take refuge in Him! Let all the upright in heart glory!

Psalm 64:10

Abide in Me, My son, and I abide in you. I am ever ready to inhabit a heart that seeks Me. I am ever ready to fellowship with a spirit who knows its need of Me. I do not look for cringing, frightened children. That image belongs to the dark side of your nature. I look for free and open communion with those who have accepted My redemption and rejoice in it. Oh, that My people could see and understand My ways! They would not come crawling as beggars, but running as little children to a loving father or mother. That is the relationship that brings joy to My heart, because it is grounded in the Truth!

November Third

This I know, that God is for me

Psalm 56:9b

Expect greater things, My child, as your faith grows. My mercy and My power are "unlimited"—meaning that greater things are no problem from My point of view. My joy is in doing good to My children. Let that thought *grow* in you—My joy is in doing good to My children. The way is open to grow in our relationship. The past is past, the future is in My hand—but its exact shape must necessarily be determined by your faith and faithfulness. Let your faith grow toward Me and My loving purpose in your life.

November Fourth

Mark the blameless man, and behold the upright, for there is posterity for the man of peace.

Psalm 37:37

Go quietly into the day. Let My peace abide in your heart. Be at peace with Me and with all you meet. This is My word of peace, My child, and I will make it a reality—if you will abide in it.

November Fifth

But because of His great love for us, God, who is rich in mercy, made us alive with Christ even when we were dead in transgressions.

Ephesians 2:4-5a NIV

The great abundance of My mercy exceeds all your needs. There is an unending and ever-flowing supply for those who turn to Me. I am the Divine Giver. It is My joy to bestow blessings—and your joy in receiving them gladdens My heart. Dwell not on the negative thoughts that arise. Quickly confess your sin and turn from it with hope quickened by My promises. The great abundance of My mercy exceeds all your needs.

November Sixth

Behold, the Lord's hand is not shortened, that it cannot save, or His ear dull, that it cannot hear; but your iniquities have made a separation between you and your God, and your sins have hid His face from you so that He does not hear.

Isaiah 59:1-2

You come to Me laden with cares. I come to you laden with peace. When you turn your cares into prayer, My peace prevails. No anxiety has room here between us, My child. No worry about yourself or others—for then you bring only your unbelief. My arm is not shortened that it cannot reach those for whom you care. My promises are not so weak that circumstances can blot them out. Cast your cares on Me. Turn them into faith-filled prayer. Rejoice in what I have already done and let your face be lightened. No room for anxiety here, My child—but faith, hope, thanksgiving and praise. I come to you laden with peace. Accept it and abide in it.

November Seventh

If you abide in Me, and My words abide in you, ask whatever you will, and it shall be done for you.

John 15:7

The word that I speak to you is My gift of love. I know your weakness and your need, and My grace bends to your cry. Fear not to call on Me, My son, for I will be entreated of you. Do not strive to think profound thoughts, and do not despise the simple ones that well up from within. Seek the wisdom of simplicity and the simplicity of wisdom. You have tasted the freshness of My living Word. Do not doubt it or neglect it. Like manna, you need it daily. It is My gift of love to you.

November Eighth

Wait for the Lord; be strong, and let your heart take courage; yea, wait for the Lord!

Psalm 27:14

The birth comes after the period of gestation. The harvest comes after the necessary period of growth and maturing. My purposes, too, await their time. I am the Lord of years. Time is My creation and serves My sovereign purpose. What seems to you delays, long delays, are merely the necessary gestation and period of maturing.

Keep your prayers alive in light of this truth. Delays are days of opportunity. Faith perceives that which the eye cannot see. Faith lays hold on My promises and does not let go. You can thus participate in My divine scheme of things, and share My joy when My purposes are fulfilled.

November Ninth

O taste and see that the Lord is good! Happy is the man who takes refuge in Him!

Psalm 34:8

Never fear to speak the word I give you. Fear will quench the free flowing of My Spirit. Boldness is needed because it always exposes you to humiliation.

It is necessary for you to venture forth with the words I give you, not knowing where they will lead or what will come next. As you can see, they *do* go "somewhere" and bring a blessing with them.

I am pleased when you calmly wait in obedience, not fretting or straining. Let your heart rest in Me, and feed your soul on the manna of My love.

November Tenth

We destroy arguments and every proud obstacle to the knowledge of God, and take every thought captive to obey Christ.

II Corinthians 10:5

As wandering sheep inevitably stray into dangerous places, the wandering mind strays into darkness. The path of light is a safe path for you, My child, but your own path is filled with briars and thorns. Has it not been so? The effort to stay in the lighted way is to *fight* the entrance of tempting thoughts. Recognizing the enemy's attempt to gain entrance into your thoughts and will is an important part of the battle. Your record here is not good. Too often you grieve My Spirit by playing the fool before his advances. Wake up to the reality that life is a battleground, and will be to the end.

November Eleventh

O Lord My God, I will give thanks to Thee for ever.

Psalm 30:12b

"Test every spirit and hold fast to that which is good." This is a true word and an important one if you are going to continue with these daily conversations. The Shepherd's Voice you should know by now, and easily recognize it when I speak. If there is confusion in your mind it is because you are resisting My word and longing for some satisfying praise.

November Twelfth

I cleave to Thy testimonies, O Lord; let me not be put to shame!

Psalm 119:31

Those who believe in Me shall never be put to shame. The adversary darkens your thoughts with the fear that you will be abandoned. But your own experience proves otherwise. Do not play the fool, My child, by believing his lies. Face this and every situation with the truth I have spoken and the truth I have supplied in your experience. Those who believe in Me *shall not* be put to shame.

November Thirteenth

The Jews had light and gladness and joy and honor.

Esther 8:16

True joy is to be found in the light. True joy is to be found in My sight. Whenever you look for it in darkness, you will find sorrow and woe. It is no accident that darkness brings on depression and sadness. It is My mercy at work, warning and guiding the soul toward its true destiny and home.

Joy in My forgiveness for past sins, My child, and learn from this consequence their true nature. Obedience is not a burden but a gateway to joy—a happy response to My holy will. Learn obedience and shun the dark impulses of your old nature—until all becomes light in My presence.

November Fourteenth

What does the Lord your God require of you, but to fear the Lord your God, to walk in all His ways, to love Him, to serve the Lord your God with all your heart and with all your soul, and to keep the commandments and statutes of the Lord, which I command you this day for your good?

Deuteronomy 10:12-13

Morning by morning I meet with you. Morning by morning I renew My assurance that you are loved. Steadiness of aim and purpose are required for the race. Victory is not to the swift nor to the strong, but to those who persevere. Any thoughts of what might lie ahead are distractions and harassment of the enemy. He attacks whenever he sees a weak, unguarded place. Be not careless or over-confident—but take care and be watchful. The battle is still joined and you must do your part.

November Fifteenth

I have loved you with an everlasting love.

Jeremiah 31:3b

I have "feasted" your soul with the rehearsal of My past words. In all of them, I have reminded you of My unfailing love. Remember that, My child, as you go through this day and this week. My love is sure and it cannot fail. There is no need that cannot be met. No prayer will go unanswered. Let love answer love and let My faithfulness steady your unsteady heart!

November Sixteenth

For He will give His angels charge of you to guard you in all your ways.
Psalm 91:11

I am keeping you, My child, I am keeping you. Think about it—how far you wandered from the path—and how mercifully I have led you back. Rehearse in your heart the milestones of My goodness. Yes, I am keeping you—I, the Lord, change not. That is your security and your rest. Only doubt and fear can rob you of that rest in Me.

November Seventeenth

O Lord, be gracious to me; heal me, for I have sinned against Thee!
Psalm 41:4

Self-inflicted wounds are the hardest to heal. This is true especially of the soul. The damage of your soul by the sin of others is little compared with what you have done. This is a long-term project, My child, and it is important that you not grow weary or discouraged. Enough that a healing is in process. The exact degree of it is not important, for what I intend is restoration and wholeness. Let patience have its perfect work, and be at peace.

November Eighteenth

Peace I leave with you; My peace I give to you; not as the world gives do I give to you. Let not your hearts be troubled, neither let them be afraid.

John 14:27

I do grant you My peace, My child, as I have promised. My peace is often hidden in the inner depths, under the turmoil of your thoughts and fears. To find My peace, you must choose to go behind and beneath those troublesome waves. Your human reasoning tells you such an abandonment of "reality" is foolish if not impossible. But I tell you that it is neither foolish nor impossible—and that true peace can only be found here. In the world you will have tribulation—the "surface" will often be turbulent. Sink beneath and discover.

November Nineteenth

Behold, Thou desirest truth in the inward being; therefore teach me wisdom in my secret heart.

Psalm 51:6

Like a patient parent I have nurtured you in these listening exercises. My tender mercies have been manifest day by day because of your great need. You do not yet know nor realize the extent and depth of your need, but I see it in its fullness, and My compassion moves to come to your aid.

There is no room for pride here—only for gratitude and love. Let your love for Me grow, My child. It is still dwarfed and shriveled beneath an overarching fear. Let love cast out fear, for it is not My will that you forever dwell in the darkness of your imagination. Let us love one another, My child, for it is My delight that we walk together in love.

November Twentieth

O Lord, my heart is not lifted up, my eyes are not raised too high; I do not occupy myself with things too great and too marvelous for me.

Psalm 131:1

The earth is the Lord's and the fullness thereof, the world and those who dwell therein. The rivers of Babylon and the waters of comfort are both Mine. The sorrows and joys, the hopes and disappointments—all are within the compass of My care.

Do not fret yourself with things too high and too hard for you. Content yourself on the reflection of My loving care—and build up the highway of a holy life lived in My will and My presence. It is not for you to know great secrets—just to live in the greatest of all wonders—My eternal, sovereign, unchangeable love!

November Twenty-first

According to His promise we wait for new heavens and a new earth in which righteousness dwells.

II Peter 3:13

It is enough that I love and care for you. It is enough that I see your tears and hear your prayers. It is enough that I have revealed to you My tender mercies. There is light enough for today's journey.

There is the bright promise of hope out before you. There is grace abounding and sufficient for every need. It is enough.

November Twenty-second

All the promises of God find their Yes in Him. That is why we utter the Amen through Him, to the glory of God.

II Corinthians 1:20

A glimpse of glory—a glimpse of My glory has been vouchsafed to you. There are yet more glorious realities to dawn, but your sight is still obscured by sin and its consequences. Yet the glimpse of glory you have seen is a lodestone to draw you toward the heavenly realm. Here you may have foretastes—but only foretastes of that which lies beyond. It is necessary to plod the mundane paths of your earthly life to prepare you for what I have prepared for you. Be of good cheer. They who put their trust in Me will not be confounded.

November Twenty-third

Depart from evil, and do good; so shall you abide for ever. For the Lord loves justice; He will not forsake His saints.

Psalm 37:27-28

No set of circumstances is beyond My sovereign power. No threat can be carried out without My permission and design to use it for good. O ye of little faith! Be at peace with Me. Let My peace rule your heart even now. I will not abandon you and leave you to your fears. Come unto Me, and I will give you heart-rest.

November Twenty-fourth

My grace is sufficient for you, for My power is made perfect in weakness.

II Corinthians 12:9

Yes, I hear and am now here. I am your strength and your hope. I am the Great Physician of your soul and body, and well acquainted with your case. Rest in the sure knowledge that grace abounds, and My power is made perfect in your weakness. You do not yet understand this, but it will become plain in My time. All is well, My child. Do not fret over the stage you are now going through.

November Twenty-fifth

God did not give us a spirit of timidity but a spirit of power and love and self-control.

II Timothy 1:7

Your doubts still hinder your obedience to My will. Your fears still lead you in the wrong direction. I call you to return in heart and mind to a greater trust in our relationship. Have you forgotten My faithfulness? Gird up your loins and quit you like a man against the enemies of your soul!

November Twenty-sixth

Unless a grain of wheat falls into the earth and dies, it remains alone; but if it dies, it bears much fruit.

John 12:24

"Except a grain of wheat fall into the ground and die, it cannot bear fruit." Falling into the ground is the hidden life to which I have called you. There, out of human sight, the secret work of My Spirit goes on. Some of it you can know consciously, but most of it is hidden even from your view. Dying is the difficult part for you, My child, because I require your consent for it to happen. I know it is hard, and My grace is abounding for you, but it is necessary if your life is to bear the harvest it was created to bring forth. Many wasted years—much "crop damage"—but there is still hope.

November Twenty-seventh

Thou hast said, "Seek ye My face." My heart says to Thee, "Thy face, Lord, do I seek." Hide not Thy face from me. Turn not Thy servant away in anger, Thou who hast been my help. Cast me not off, forsake me not, O God of my salvation!

Psalm 27:8-9

There are no easy answers to the perplexities you face. There is only one answer—My sovereign grace. As light emerges from the east and lightens the whole sky, so My grace "with healing in its wings" comes to you. The perplexities remain—but you do not have to be bound to them nor in them. They are smaller than they seem, and much less powerful than they appear. The light of grace will help you see them more clearly.

November Twenty-eighth

Whatever you ask in prayer, you will receive, if you have faith.

Matthew 21:22

Expect greater things, My child, from My hand. Do not limit your prayers with puny faith, but *believe* so that I hear and answer your heart-felt prayers.

November Twenty-ninth

Trust in the Lord with all your heart, and do not rely on your own insight.

Proverbs 3:5

Do not seek to understand all mysteries. Thereby many have been led astray. Let the mystery remain—a wonder and a reminder that you are not God. I am He who reveals the secrets in their time. I disclose that which, in My wisdom, is best. Be content to live in the incomplete—with unanswered questions and puzzlements that you cannot decipher. In this way your soul will grow in My likeness—and that is what I will for you.

November Thirtieth

He leads the humble in what is right, and teaches the humble His way.
Psalm 25:9

This is My word today. Carry out the gentle nudges and quiet thoughts that come to you. Do not allow your disbelief to rob you of My intended blessing. Nothing else can hinder it. Believe, act, and see.

DECEMBER

Jesus, Thou divine Companion,
 By Thy lowly human birth
Thou hast come to join the workers,
 Burden-bearers of the earth.
Thou, the carpenter of Nazareth,
 Toiling for Thy daily food,
By Thy patience and Thy courage,
 Thou hast taught us toil is good.

Where the many toil together,
 There art Thou among Thine own;
Where the tired workman sleepeth,
 There art Thou with him alone;
Thou, the peace that passeth knowledge,
 Dwellest in the daily strife;
Thou, the Bread of heaven, art broken
 In the sacrament of life.

Every task, however simple,
 Sets the soul that does it free;
Every deed of love and kindness
 Done to man is done to Thee.
Jesus, Thou divine Companion,
 Help us all to work our best;
Bless us in our daily labor,
 Lead us to our Sabbath rest.

Henry van Dyke, 1909

December First

Through Thy precepts I get understanding; therefore I hate every false way.

Psalm 119:104

Let go the false dreams you have cherished—they are idols of wood. Let go their hold on your heart so that you may be open to My plans and purpose. Your inward resistance brings much unneeded suffering and robs you and others of My proffered joy and fulfillment. False dreams are false gods that rob My people of their inheritance. Don't play the fool, My child.

December Second

Do not hide Thy face from me in the day of my distress! Incline Thy ear to me; answer me speedily in the day when I call!

Psalm 102:2

Yes, My child, I will answer. The prayers you pray are not in vain. They become a part of My provision for blessing. They become servants, instruments of My peace. Be at peace with them, and choose to rest your heart in the surety of My promise. I have heard and I will answer.

December Third

But of that day and hour no one knows, not even the angels of heaven, nor the Son, but the Father only. Therefore you also must be ready; for the Son of man is coming at an hour you do not expect.

Matthew 24:36, 44

The mystery of My coming will always remain. It is not yours to understand but to receive. It is hidden for My purpose and in My purpose. Expect that I will come to you, My child, in My own time and way—bringing blessing and the gift of Myself. Do not think, wrongly, that it is a light gift. Keep watching and expecting—till I come.

December Fourth

I go to prepare a place for you. . . . I will come again and will take you to Myself, that where I am you may be also.

John 14:2b, 3

Don't give up! Don't give in! The small growth in your perception of My love for you can encourage you to persevere in the path I am placing before you. Remember, My child, that I take "the long view" in our walk together. What you cannot see or imagine is crystal-clear to Me, and so I bear with you in your struggles. Your failures are less disturbing to Me than to you. So don't give up! Don't give in! The struggles are worth more than gold because they move you along the path. You will not be disappointed.

December Fifth

Everyone who is of the truth hears My voice.

John 18:37c

My child, I often speak to you in quiet tones, but My voice is drowned by your busy thoughts. You must learn, as you have begun to learn, to *listen*. My Spirit is life and brings life. Your spirit has no life of itself. I shall not leave you until I have accomplished that which I have begun in you. Be prepared to change. Do not be afraid. Already the hour is late, but there is ample time. Be sensitive to the leading that comes, checking your old habits and patterns of thought, action and reaction. Hunger and thirst for more of Me, of My life and My way. Even now the old is passing away, and will pass—if you will let it go. You do not have to understand—only trust—and see My glory revealed. O My child, do you not see the wonder of My love?

December Sixth

Let me hear in the morning of Thy steadfast love, for in Thee I put my trust. Teach me the way I should go, for to Thee I lift up my soul.
Psalm 143:8

My Spirit I have given to abide in you and to guide you into all truth. My truth is too large for your limited mind, and sometimes you meet what seems to be contradictions. These confuse you and confound your arrogant self-righteousness. You remember how you struggled with the accounts of the Resurrection many years ago—and suffered because you could not make them "match up." Even then, I was dealing with one of your most serious sins—your demand to understand everything in "black and white." This was meant to humble you and to quiet your incessant yearning to understand all mysteries.

Your life now is full of mysteries you cannot explain. I have surrounded you with many things for which your heart longed from childhood. Remember that as you enjoy the unfolding of the beauty of My world. I saw and felt the yearning you knew, and in My love and grace, I have "satisfied the desire" of your spirit. Receive these tokens of My goodness and let them bring new depths of gratitude to your heart. Do you see how these gifts are also dimensions of My truth! There are wonders yet to be unfolded. Trust and follow your Guide.

December Seventh

Since all have sinned and fall short of the glory of God, they are justi-fied by His grace as a gift, through the redemption which is in Christ Jesus.

Romans 3:23-24

My dear child, mourn your sins but rejoice in My saving love. Repent of all that is in you that resists and rebels against My will. But rejoice that My grace is all-sufficient—even for you. Your proud and arrogant nature pollutes much of your relationship with others and with Me. It separates and isolates you from true communion and true fellowship. Add to that your memories of past sins and hurts, and you are rendered incapable of doing laudable service—except for My over-ruling grace. The more you see and recognize this, the freer you will become to move into a grace-filled life. You are still choosing, too often, the old paths. They are death. Choose life. To live you must die to the old and embrace the "giving up" of its tem-porary satisfactions—however costly the "giving up" may appear. Let them win! Give up your demand to be accepted and recognized. Hide yourself internally in My side. Do it in love, not in self-pity or vindictiveness—allow Me to become your All.

December Eighth

For the word of God is living and active, sharper than any two-edged sword, piercing to the division of soul and spirit, of joints and marrow, and discerning the thoughts and intentions of the heart.

Hebrews 4:12

Relax, My child, and do not be anxious. Today is planned and tomorrow. You have only to stay in a receiving attitude to be blessed. I do not require of My children more than they are able to bring before Me. This includes your ability to stay your mind and chase away vain thoughts. When I say "relax," I do not invite you to be slovenly or presumptuous—but to be at peace in My presence. Herein is love. Herein is home.

December Ninth

What I have vowed I will pay.

Jonah 2:9b

It is enough for you to know that I am with you. Every day is a new revelation of My unchanging love and mercy. You do not need new "facts" or information about the future. That would only satisfy your pride and put temptation in your way. I deal with you in keeping with what I know you to be—and My way is perfect. You have everything you need for today. Let your gratitude be commensurate with the gift.

December Tenth

"Lord, how often shall my brother sin against me, and I forgive him? As many as seven times?" Jesus said to him, "I do not say to you seven times, but seventy times seven."

Matthew 18:21b-22

My yoke is easy and My burden is light. I impose no harsh duties on My children. The hardest lesson for you to learn is My gentleness. Your own harsh nature reflects the attitude of today's psalm: the desire to see your "enemy" suffer. Such satisfaction is short-lived, and brings its own bitterness with it. You have the opportunity in your present life situation to bear My easy yoke and learn of Me. Learn to forgive. Learn to forgive. Learn how light a burden I ask you to bear. Unforgiveness is a heavy one—and unnecessary.

December Eleventh

I will sing aloud of Thy steadfast love in the morning. O my Strength, I will sing praises to Thee, for Thou, O God, art my fortress, the God who shows me steadfast love.

Psalm 59:16a, 17

Go into this day with the full assurance of My love. Let no cloud of doubt stand between us, for My heart is open to you. Your faith is small and weak, and your wounds are many. But I am with you to bind up, cheer up, and raise up a soul to My glory.

December Twelfth

God, the Lord, who created the heavens and stretched them out, who spread forth the earth and what comes from it, who gives breath to the people upon it and spirit to those who walk in it.

Isaiah 42:5

Look and listen, My child. By these two methods you will learn. See Me more clearly in My wondrous works. See the grandeur of My purposes. I am God who created all this universe to My glory and to the good of My children. So look! Admire My handiwork, and let your heart expand its capacity for wonder and praise. Do not look just at the created, material world. Look at the interweaving of circumstances, the evidence of My presence and providence behind the ordinary events. You are still too blind! Look! For your soul's health, learn.

It is good that you are *learning* to listen. It is good that you are *learning* to trust My word to you. Healing is going on inside you, and I want that to continue. But you must cooperate. It is not automatic, and it will not be forced on you. Keep listening, My child. The wonder will grow.

December Thirteenth

The Lord sees not as man sees; man looks on the outward appearance, but the Lord looks on the heart.

I Samuel 16:7b

You have always tried to appear better than you know yourself to be. My aim is to bring reality into what you tried to appear to be. Others were not fooled by your projection of yourself—at least not all of them. This was and is My safeguard against your plunging into fatal delusion and hypocrisy.

To achieve My goal and purpose in your life requires painful recognition of the seriousness of your sins and the continued cleansing that I will effect in response to your deep repentance. No one else can do this for you—it is between you and Me. It requires not only sorrow for the past, but a watchful care over your thought-life in the present and the future. Guard it well, My child. Guard it well!

December Fourteenth

The fear of the Lord is hatred of evil. Pride and arrogance and the way of evil and perverted speech I hate.

Proverbs 8:13

My son, do not worry about differences of opinions and understandings between you and others. Do not lose your peace or become argumentative in your mind or manner. Remember what I said to you before: Let them win. Let their way prevail—for the danger to you is greater than the danger of error. Pride has much to do with the strength of your convictions. Therefore pride must "take a beating"—and be put down. Rejoice that this is so. The pain becomes less as you cooperate in the process.

These things are not central. They do not destroy the gospel. Hold fast to what you have received. Treasure My words and My Word. Feed on My Word more and more, and you will be able to rest in Me. That is the path I have laid out for you. It is a good path. Accept it and let *pride* die.

December Fifteenth

For you have need of endurance; so that you may do the will of God and receive what is promised.

Hebrews 10:36

My dear child, do not forget My mercies to you. The remembrance of them is a safeguard against your nature. The remembrance is also a foundation for your expectant hope. My mercy has rescued you from many a dangerous situation—where your adversary and Mine would have destroyed you. Yes, I mean "*destroyed* you" like a lion seizing its prey and devouring it. I rescued you from the lion's paw. Remember that and take heart!

December Sixteenth

For the sake of your tradition, you have made void the word of God.

Matthew 15:6

Today I call you to listen more intently and faithfully to My voice. You are still too full of your own voice, and you ignore Me many, many times every day. I want you to learn to hear the still, small voice above the "storms of passion and self-will." This is particularly needful in your conversations with others, where you hope to make points, be clever, or get your opinion accepted. Be *still* before Me. Learn to listen in the activity of conversing. There is still plenty of room to listen.

December Seventeenth

If this plan or this undertaking is of men, it will fail; but if it is of God, you will not be able to overthrow them. You might even be found opposing God!

Acts 5:38b-39

My good will ever wills and seeks your good. When your will and My will are in unity, only good can flow from it. When your will is contrary to My will, I still work for good—in spite of your resistance. The sooner your will lines up with My will, the sooner the suffering and conflict can cease.

Flowing from My throne on high in never-ending, full supply, abundant grace and power divine, for every chosen child of Mine.

December Eighteenth

I waited patiently for the Lord; He inclined to me and heard my cry.

Psalm 40:1

You wait to hear My word. Remember, My child, how long I have waited for you. Remember My patient perseverance as your mind was led in strange and vain paths. Yes, I waited for your return, knowing that a seed of faith had been planted in you. You must also be patient and persevering in awaiting My visitation. Think not that this exercise is in vain, for I never arrive too late. Let My word be an encouragement to you in the days ahead, when delay seems long. Persevere.

December Nineteenth

"Before the cock crows today, you will deny Me three times." And he went out and wept bitterly.

Luke 22:61b-62

The beauty you see is but a dim reflection of what is to be. It is a flawed beauty, because My world is a flawed world. Sin and rebellion leave their marks everywhere. Yet I give glimpses of truth and inner visions of beauty to the souls that seek them. Beware that you do not become captive to the flawed vision. The old is passing and will pass away. Awake to the new that is to come and embrace the changes in your life by which it draws nearer. Your salvation is nearer than when you first believed.

December Twentieth

You will seek Me and find Me, when you seek Me with all your heart.
                                                                    Jeremiah 29:13

You are coming to the feast of My humiliation. It is not that I was humbled by men, but that I chose this path of My own sovereign will. No shame clung to the circumstances, because it was My loving, saving purpose behind it. You can rid yourself of false shame in your humiliations if you will learn from Me. At the present time, you still carry this unnecessary burden and it hampers your witness to My mercy in your life. Despise the shame, My son— and accept My gracious dealings—including your humiliations.

December Twenty-first

Blessed are those who are invited to the marriage supper of the lamb. These are true words of God.

Revelation 19:9

The thoughts that I give you carry with them the seed of life. They may seem quite ordinary, but their quality is hidden within. You shall know the truth of this more and more as time goes on. I want you to be more responsive to these thoughts and to respect them more highly. Your stubborn will resists Me and this hinders your progress greatly. Pray specifically that My will shall prevail over yours, and that My thoughts will "expel" yours.

December Twenty-second

The sum of Thy word is truth; and every one of Thy righteous ordinances endures for ever.

Psalm 119:160

All My words are truth and all have life in them. The reason you look forward to them is that they enliven your spirit. This is a mystery to you, but it is reality.

My word today is to cease not to pray. The subtle snares of Satan still remain, and without prayer you are no match for him. Do not overestimate your strength. Do not presume on My rescuing grace. I expect you to become a faithful warrior in the spiritual fight. Your record is not good. You are too ready to "check out" and escape the conflict. Arm yourself and be not fearful—the battle is won when My people pray.

December Twenty-third

Come to Me, all who labor and are heavy laden, and I will give you rest. Take My yoke upon you, and learn from Me; for I am gentle and lowly in heart, and you will find rest for your souls. For My yoke is easy, and My burden is light.

Matthew 11:28-30

I have heard your prayer, My child, I never turn a deaf ear to My children. I am not such a one as you, nor as you perceive Me to be. You do not yet know or fathom the depth of My love. Your proud nature, though wounded by many blows, by My permission, still distorts your vision of Me. I am meek and lowly in heart, and here—in My merciful presence—you shall find rest unto your soul. Where is boasting here? Where is glory? Where is calculation of merits and good works? Where is condemnation? Not here—not any of these things. None are relevant when you enter this place of rest. I am here—the meek and lowly one. I am here—He who forgiveth your iniquities and healeth your diseases. I am here—your health and salvation. And when you turn—truly turn to Me—do you not realize that My love is satisfied, and the travail of My soul is satisfied in that turning? For this I suffered. For this I died—that you might turn to Me and know how much you are loved. Don't be afraid of My love. Don't hesitate to turn to Me.

December Twenty-fourth

No man has ever seen God; if we love one another, God abides in us and His love is perfected in us.

I John 4:12

Today I am showing you the wideness of My mercy. Open your eyes to behold My generous and tender heart. Hidden from the "wise" and worldly spirit, My movements are within the human soul. They are in very truth "underground" movements, but the results and fruit become visible in due time.

I will be with you in your obedient answer to My call. The appointment is not an accident. It is by My design and for My purpose. Do not let that fact make you proud, but let it humble you before My face. Be yourself. I have prepared you through many a cross, to free you to bring My word to others with life. Trust Me and let Me bless you, also.

December Twenty-fifth

After this I will return, and I will rebuild the dwelling of David, which has fallen; I will rebuild its ruins, and I will set it up, that the rest of men may seek the Lord.

Acts 15:16-17a

Vain regrets are vanity. They are empty clouds bearing no water and no life. Many decisions in the past were wrong and carried with them seeds of suffering. Some of that suffering is in seeking consequences undreamed of—and bitter. Vain regret cannot change the past. The seeds of suffering germinate and grow, bringing their inevitable fruit. Without Me this would be a tragic tale—and life would, indeed, be sad.

But I am the Lord who builds on ruins. Sometimes ruins are the only material I can use, and all that was promising and beautiful must be allowed to crumble and fall before the real work of lasting beauty can rise. Look well at the fruit of folly, the pain of plans and dreams gone awry. Then look to Me, at what I am doing—yes, I the Lord am doing a new thing. In every situation where the seed of suffering is flowering and bearing fruit, I am at work on the ruins. Keep looking, and your sorrow will turn to joy in the morning.

December Twenty-sixth

Thy statutes have been my songs in the house of my pilgrimage. I remember Thy name in the night, O Lord, and keep Thy law. This blessing has fallen to me, that I have kept Thy precepts.

Psalm 119:54-56

My dear child, do not forget all My benefits—the innumerable blessings I have poured on your pilgrimage. Some of them were hard for you to understand and accept. You fought against them and even rejected some. But many came unbidden and undeserved—blessings that accepted with little thought of the divine kindness that sent them. These times of communion are a refreshment and renewal of memory of these blessings. My blessings display My love—but My love goes far beyond the "benefits" for which you are rightly to give praise. They are the "edges of My ways." So praise My kindness in these blessings and be prepared to love Me beyond the benefits.

December Twenty-seventh

It is the spirit that gives life, the flesh is of no avail; the words that I have spoken to you are spirit and life.

John 6:63

Quiet your soul before Me, and I will speak. Your usual chatter drowns out the still, small voice of My Spirit. Do not be afraid of inner quiet. I am your Protector and Defender. Be *still* and know. Be *still* and hear. Be *still* and experience the wonders of My love and grace. I wait to be gracious—yes, I, the Lord, *wait* for My children to still their own voices that they may hear Mine. You, My child, still have a long way to go to learn to do this readily and easily. Your chatter is really mental clutter. Let Me help you become more *unclut-tered*—and thus more at peace with yourself and with Me. *My* peace I give to you—when and as you are prepared to accept it.

December Twenty-eighth

Great peace have those who love Thy law; nothing can make them stumble.

Psalm 119:165

I am your Peace. It is My Presence that brings you a sense of security and well-being. It is My gift to you—a "clear shining after rain." Let gratitude grow and keep looking up to Me for further mercies. Your need can never outrun My supply. These are primary, "first-grade" lessons, but you need them rehearsed over and over again. Do not forget to be grateful and generous. I am your Peace today.

December Twenty-ninth

I formed you, you are My servant; O Israel, you will not be forgotten by Me. . . . Return to Me, for I have redeemed you.

Isaiah 44:21b-22

In the womb of the morning new life is begotten. My Spirit quickens and brings life anew. Doubt not that it is so, but throw off the old and put on that newness I bring.

December Thirtieth

God will ransom my soul from the power of Sheol.

Psalm 49:15

Every word of Mine is established in the heavens. There are no idle thoughts, no empty, lifeless sounds. When I speak to you, My son, there is always purpose and power in what I say. Because you are still "in kindergarten" spiritually, My words remain on that level for your sake. Do not despise or doubt them. They are not empty thoughts, but are filled with My purpose and power. Time will tell.

December Thirty-first

What does the Lord your God require of you? Only to walk in all His ways, to love Him, to serve the Lord your God with all your heart and with all your soul . . . for your own well being.

Deuteronomy 10:12-13

Continue on in the path, My son. It is a good path, and leads onward toward our mutual goal. Calm your fears, child. I am here and will be here always and all the way.

Deo Gratias